A to Z of Critical Thinking

Also available from Continuum:

Critical Thinking: An Introduction to Reasoning Well, Jamie Carlin Watson
and Robert Arp
A to Z of Philosophy, Alexander Moseley

A to Z of Critical Thinking

Edited by
Beth Black

Contributing Authors
Anne Thomson
John Butterworth
Joe Chislett
Beth Black
Geoff Willis
Jacquie Thwaites

CAMBRIDGE **ASSESSMENT**

UNIVERSITY *of* CAMBRIDGE
Local Examinations Syndicate

continuum

Continuum International Publishing Group

The Tower Building　　　　　　80 Maiden Lane
11 York Road　　　　　　　　　Suite 704
London SE1 7NX　　　　　　　　New York NY 10038

www.continuumbooks.com

British Library Cataloguing-in-Publication Data
A catalogue record for this book is available from the British Library.

ISBN: HB: 978-0-8264-2055-8
　　　 PB: 978-1-4411-1797-7

Library of Congress Cataloging-in-Publication Data
A catalog record of this book is available from the Library of Congress.

Typeset by Newgen Imaging Systems Pvt Ltd, Chennai, India
Printed and bound in India.

To Tom Bramley, Sylvia Green, Tim Oates and,
of course, Beatrix.

Contents

Foreword

Thinking Skills, and more specifically, Critical Thinking, are often noted as important ingredients of the school experience – essential skills for the knowledge age. But Critical Thinking, possibly more than many discipline areas, is one in which there are problems of definition. There are various reasons for it. There are 'false friends' whereby the meaning of everyday usage of a term might differ subtly from a more technical usage (cf 'argument', 'dilemma'). Other definitional problems have perhaps arisen because two concepts are closely related and therefore easily confused (cf flawed arguments versus unsound arguments; consistency and coherence); or even because they do genuinely overlap and converge (cf circular argument and begging the question, fallacy and flaw). And some concepts are genuinely mercurial (arguably, the term 'Critical Thinking' is a good example here!). Thus, the aim of this glossary is to provide authoritative clarification and disambiguation of the terms and concepts that are the tools of good thinking.

The glossary represents the culmination of a longer programme of work in Critical Thinking, which has included deriving a definition and taxonomy of Critical Thinking (Black et al., 2008) and exploring how the discipline is taught in schools (Black, 2009). A public debate of the nature and value of Critical Thinking was hosted by Cambridge Assessment at the British Academy, London in February 2010.

We hope that students, teachers, academics and anyone wishing to hone their thinking will find some advantage in reading this book. In general, each entry consists of a short definition followed by a more detailed explanation, often with the use of interesting and illuminating examples. Where appropriate, there is discussion of the differences between the definition in hand and other, related terms. Terms in small capitals or in capitals and small capitals indicate there is a separate entry in the book. Finally, the reader is directed to other related terms not mentioned in the body of the text.

Simon Lebus
Chief Executive of Cambridge Assessment
February 2011

Further reading

Black, B. (2009), '"It's not like teaching other subjects" – the challenges of introducing Critical Thinking AS level in England'. Research Matters 10, A Cambridge Assessment publication, 2–8.

Abduction

reasoning that, because a hypothesis has explanatory power, it is (therefore) true – or at least probable. This kind of reasoning also goes by the names of argument to the best explanation and hypothetical induction.

Inference to the best explanation is a very common form of reasoning. Indeed, we probably all reason in this way many times a day, often hardly aware of doing so. Suppose, for instance, I hear a knock on the door at the time when the postman normally delivers parcels. I assume that it *is* the postman at the door just because this *would* explain the knock.

More seriously, suppose a doctor examines a patient and discovers a whole range of symptoms that *would* be explained *if* the patient had condition X. The doctor infers that the patient *does* have condition X. This is abduction.

The problem with the method is that often there are several PLAUSIBLE explanations which could equally be true. Moreover, the most obvious explanation is not always the best one, nor the right one.

There is a famous Welsh legend which illustrates how abduction can go badly wrong:

> In the 13th century Llewelyn, prince of North Wales, was out hunting, for once without his faithful hound, Gelert. On Llewelyn's return the dog, stained and smeared with blood, joyfully sprang to meet his master. The prince hastened to find his son, and saw the infant's cot empty, the bedclothes and floor covered with blood. The frantic father plunged his sword into the hound's side, thinking it had killed his heir. The dog's dying yell was answered by a child's cry.
>
> Llewelyn searched and discovered his boy unharmed, but nearby lay the body of a mighty wolf which Gelert had slain. The prince, filled with remorse, is said never to have smiled again.
>
> (From the headstone at Gelert's grave, Beddgelert, North Wales)

Nonetheless, inference to the best explanation, used intelligently, is a powerful reasoning tool, especially in science. Think, for example, of the way the theory of gravity *explains* the rise and fall of tides or the orbits of the planets; or how the theory of natural selection explains the diversity of living organisms. We can infer from the fact that these theories offer plausible and convincing explanations for many different phenomena that (therefore) the theories have a strong likelihood of being correct.

See also: EXPLANATION and INDUCTION.

Ad hoc

brought in for the purpose.

An ad hoc move in reasoning is when a claim or premise is added for no other reason than to defend the argument from challenges or difficulties. The immediate and intended result of the ad hoc move is that the original belief or argument can be accommodated after all. Suppose, for example, a politician was arguing that all forms of gambling are undesirable. It is pointed out to him that he has expressed support for the introduction of the national lottery. On being reminded of this he responds that all forms of gambling, *except when they are state-run*, are undesirable. That would be an ad hoc move, and it would weaken his original argument.

The distinguished Victorian naturalist Philip Gosse, responded to Darwin's theory of evolution in a famously ad hoc manner. He was a member of the Plymouth Brethren and accepted unconditionally a literal interpretation of the creation story in Genesis. However, he needed to respond to the fossil evidence which appeared to show that life forms of increasing complexity developed over time. He was too well informed to reject the fossil record out of hand. So instead, he squared his literal belief in creationism with an acceptance of the fossil record by adding the third, ad hoc, claim that God had created fossils in this order as a test of faith. This is clearly ad hoc reasoning.

See also: FLAW, COUNTER-EXAMPLE and POST HOC AND ERGO PROPTER HOC.

Ad hominem

Latin for 'at, or towards, the man', this is an attempt to weaken the opposing position by directing your attack at the person who put forward the argument rather than at his or her argument.

The truth of a claim is logically independent of its origins; put another way, the competence or credibility of a person has no relevance to the truth of what they say. The following passage contains two examples of an ad hominem attack:

> In a recent House of Commons debate, many MPs argued against giving prisoners the right to vote. The main reasons supplied reflected concerns that serious criminals (e.g. rapists, paedophiles, axe-murderers etc.) should be granted the right to help choose the next MPs. To support this view, some MPs pointed out that John Hirst, the person who started the campaign to give prisoners the right to vote, is himself a convicted axe-murderer. However, one MP stood up in favour of giving prisoners these basic civic rights, asking for a return to 'classic, do-gooding, bleeding-heart British liberalism'. But he was criticised as merely being a controversialist.

Certainly, the CREDIBILITY of a claim *is* affected by its source. However, just as it is fallacious to assume that because an expert holds a particular view, the view must be correct (see, APPEAL TO AUTHORITY/EXPERTISE), it is also fallacious to assume that because someone lacks credibility, the claim must therefore be false. Moreover, if the person has provided reasons for the claim, but these reasons are not considered on the grounds that the arguer lacks credibility, then what was a relevant attack becomes ad hominem. (If it is not the conclusion but the reasons themselves, or an individual claim which is being objected to, then the 'attack' is often more relevant – 'We should not trust her statement entirely as she is clearly biased on this issue' see, CREDIBILITY). However, dismissing someone's whole argument on the grounds that they lack credibility on an issue, without even considering what they say, is a clear case of flawed ad hominem reasoning.)

Not all critical references directed 'to the person' *are* fallacious. For instance, if I accuse someone of hypocrisy or inconsistency on the grounds that in the past they have said or done something that warrants this claim, then I am arguing ad hominem but not necessarily committing a FALLACY. The person's record in such a case is germane and arguing from it is legitimate.

Affirming the consequent

See: FALLACY FORMAL and NECESSARY AND SUFFICIENT CONDITIONS.

Allegation

type of claim which asserts something without proof.

Calling something an allegation reminds us that the truth of the claim has not yet been established. Referring to an assertion as an 'allegation' should alert the audience to the fact that the claim is as yet unproved.

See also: CLAIM and ASSERTION.

Ambiguity

the characteristic of having more than one possible meaning.

Ambiguity differs from VAGUENESS (lack of precision in language) in that an ambiguous word or statement has two or more possible meanings that are clearly discernible, yet it is not possible, without further information or context, to decide which meaning is intended.

For example, the following statements are ambiguous:

Lilia left her toy rabbit behind when she went to see the doctor.

This could mean either that Lilia left her rabbit in the place she was in before she went to see the doctor, or that she left her rabbit behind at the doctor's when she left.

The cat had a fight with the dog and injured its paw.

In this case it is not clear whether the cat's or the dog's paw was injured.

It is wrong to claim that the Leader of the Opposition was lying.

This may mean that it factually incorrect (i.e. untrue) that the Leader of the Opposition was lying, or it may mean that it is morally wrong to accuse the Leader of the Opposition of lying.

Thinking critically about arguments that involve ambiguity requires identification of the possible meanings, and evaluation of the argument in relation to each of those meanings.

See also: CLARIFYING MEANING, EQUIVOCATION and VAGUENESS.

Analogy (argument from)

a comparison, the purpose of which is to either persuade or explain.

argument from analogy – an argument based partly or exclusively on a comparison.

When explaining or clarifying, analogies tend to work by finding a similar (analogous) situation that the person is likely to be more familiar with, in order to clarify, or demystify, the idea or concept being explained. Analogies are used when the idea being explained is difficult or abstract; in science, for example, analogies are often used to explain difficult concepts about things that are hard to visualize, perhaps because they are very large or very small. For example, a teacher of geology, in order to help students understand how short a time modern humans have been around (approximately 200,000 years) in relation to the magnitude of geologic time (approximately 4,600,000,000 years since the beginnings of the Earth) might liken the relative periods of existence to just a single day, where the Earth was formed at 0000 hrs and 00 seconds; and humankind only appeared at 2359 hours and 22 seconds.

Note that an analogy differs from a 'model' in that the things being compared are deliberately different, but share one or more (essentially) similar features. A model is a representation of the thing it is explaining.

Of most interest to Critical Thinking are the analogies which play an argumentative or persuasive role, when the analogy is being used to support or justify a point – that is, in arguments from analogy. In these analogies it is hoped that the similarity or similarities between the two things being compared are such that, what is true of (the relevant feature of) one case will also be true of (relevant feature of) the other case. For instance:

> Just as sports need rules so that everyone can compete fairly with each other, businesses need regulations in order to keep competition fair and genuine. Therefore there need to be clear regulations in place that all businesses have to abide by.

The argument is not suggesting that sports are like businesses in every respect; merely that they are similar from the point of view of needing some binding rules to keep the competition 'fair and genuine'.

The following is also an argument from analogy:

> People worry that the growth of supermarkets will necessarily lead to the death of specialist shops such as butchers and fishmongers. But in France the small shops have survived despite the appearance of large supermarkets. If the two can co-exist in France, then there's no reason why they shouldn't also be able to here.

Here the analogy is between two similar situations, but in different places.

As these two examples show, it is not necessarily the case that the more similar the things being compared (in a general sense) the more effective the analogy. A good analogy is where the two things are closely alike in the relevant respects. In fact, from a persuasive point of view, often the more unlike the two things are, the more effective the analogy:

> Religion is the opium of the masses.
> (Karl Marx)

Here, Marx was asserting that dependency upon religion is similar to the effects of dependency upon opium, and in particular in that both create 'illusory happiness'.

An important point to make about arguments from analogy is that, however persuasive they may be (in part, owing to their rhetorical force), they can never offer conclusive support for their conclusions. Yet at the same time they can often have a persuasive power that goes beyond the actual strength of the analogy itself – through, for example, the colourfulness or wittiness of the comparison, or the connotations of the things being compared. For these reasons, arguments from analogy are notoriously difficult to evaluate.

See also: APPEAL TO HISTORY/PRECEDENT and RHETORICAL LANGUAGE.

Analysis

breaking something down into its constituent parts, usually in order to under-stand it and/or explain it. In Critical Thinking the most important application of analysis is in connection with ARGUMENT.

Analysing a simple argument means identifying its constituent parts, namely REASONS (PREMISES) and CONCLUSION, and revealing its structure by showing how the parts relate to each other.

Here is a simple argument followed by a basic analysis:

Text:

Parrots are carnivorous. You can tell this from the fact that a parrot has a hooked beak, and all carnivores have hooked beaks.

Analysis:

R_1: A parrot has a hooked beak.

R_2: All carnivores have hooked beaks.

C: Parrots are carnivorous.

R_1 and R_2 are reasons (premises); C is the conclusion.

Analysis needs to be distinguished from EVALUATION. Evaluation determines whether or not an argument is sound, valid, successful and so forth. The above argument, for instance, is none of these as it is seriously flawed, but analysis on its own will not reveal this. The role of analysis is to establish that a text is an argument, or can be understood as an argument, and to identify its parts and structure. It is thus a precursor to evaluation which goes on to judge whether or not the argument succeeds.

However, argument analysis is not simply a mechanical process; it often involves some interpretation. In the example above the argument structure is very clear and unmistakable, but texts in natural discourse – for example, journalism – may have two or more plausible interpretations, and the critic's task is to decide which one to adopt. When this is the case we should employ what is known as the 'PRINCIPLE OF CHARITY' which, simply stated, means looking for the best, most logical or rational, interpretation. That may mean deciding that the text is not an argument at all.

See also: ARGUMENT STRUCTURE and EXTRACTING AN ARGUMENT.

Anecdotal evidence

Anecdotal evidence is evidence based on a limited number of reported experiences or observations – sometimes no more than one. Arguments which use anecdotal evidence to make broad generalizations are liable to be fallacious.

An example of anecdotal evidence:

> Birmingham is a crime-ridden city. Both times I've been there I've been mugged.

The 'anecdotes' are the two muggings. Although these anecdotes are evidence that muggings can occur in Birmingham, they are not adequate grounds for the conclusion that the city is 'crime-ridden'. I might go to Birmingham another hundred times without getting mugged again.

This should not be taken to mean there are no inferences which can reliably be drawn from anecdotal evidence. The following argument is *not* fallacious because it does not overgeneralize:

Letters sent by first class post do not always arrive the next working day. I have known several letters that have taken up to three days to arrive.

But by the same token, its conclusion (the first sentence) is very weak – that is, very limited. What can be inferred from this is that strong conclusions – for example, generalizations – need strong supporting evidence, and therefore anecdotal evidence tends to be inadequate.

Note that in this context an 'anecdote' does not have to be a personal experience. The next example also employs anecdotal evidence:

Three separate accounts have been received of grey wolves being sighted on Scottish farms. Farmers need to take urgent action to avoid harm to their livestock.

(This time it is left to the reader to decide whether or not the evidence justifies the conclusion.)

See also: GENERALIZATION and EXAMPLES.

Appeals

group term for a range of extremely common arguing techniques. Most notable examples are Appeals to Popularity, Authority, Emotion and History/Tradition.

In many cases, appeals are little more than persuasive devices, that, when analysed, offer little or no rational support. This is especially true of appeals to emotion (and especially appeals to anger, pity or fear), popularity and often authority. Some appeals, however, can be legitimate. The fact that an argument makes use of an appeal is not *necessarily* a sign of weakness. Some appeals are more relevant than others, and an element of care is needed when responding to appeals for this reason (see, individual entries on the different appeals). Since they are more often than not lacking in providing genuine (rational) support, when the term is used it is assumed to have a negative meaning unless it is qualified (e.g. 'The argument makes an appeal to authority which is warranted because. . .' or 'The arguer appeals to popularity but in this case the appeal is relevant because. . .'); if it was said of an argument that it contained an appeal to popularity, with no further comment, this would naturally be taken to mean the argument made an unfair, or illegitimate, appeal.

Since there are many different appeals, it is difficult to form a general rule that covers the use or recognition of all of them. The label 'appeals to' could just as accurately be replaced with 'reference to' or 'reliance upon'. The idea is that 'support' is provided for a claim that is partly or wholly irrelevant on logical grounds, but which often creates the impression or illusion of support.

Appeals often function on an emotional level. People instinctively trust and respect experts. People naturally fear and respect authority. People naturally are influenced by consensus views and behaviour. For the fact that appeals are so persuasive and yet in most cases largely irrational, recognizing appeals, and discerning between good appeals and bad, is an important skill in Critical Thinking. (Note that appeals are used with the intention to either give direct support to the conclusion of an argument or, to help establish one or more of the premises.)

See also: APPEAL TO AUTHORITY/EXPERTISE, APPEAL TO EMOTION/PITY/ANGER/FEAR ETC., APPEAL TO HISTORY/PRECEDENT, APPEAL TO POPULARITY and APPEAL TO TRADITION.

Appeal to authority/expertise

the reference to a figure or body of authority, or expertise, that concurs with the claim or view contended, in order to argue or imply that the claim or view is therefore correct, or worthy of serious consideration.

Appealing to authority is the Critical Thinking equivalent of name-dropping. 'If a great thinker such as Plato thinks that there is nothing wrong with slavery, then perhaps we shouldn't see it in such a negative light'. If someone were to use this claim to try to justify the use of slavery, they would be guilty of an appeal to authority. This is because they have not presented Plato's reasons, merely his viewpoint; moreover it is assumed that because he is a great thinker, his view is (likely to be) correct.

Appeals to authority (and to some extent expertise) appeal to our natural inclination to believe that (some) other people know better than us, and therefore if they think something we ought to think the same, or if they claim something we ought to agree with them. As with the other APPEALS, there may be a degree of intimidation or bullying in this approach to persuasion (see, also, APPEAL TO POPULARITY). The fact that a person of substance or status holds a particular view does not make that view correct; nor does it constitute a conclusive reason for agreeing with it.

As can be seen with the given example, the term 'authority' is used very loosely: it does not necessarily mean in any official sense (although this may well be the case, especially in more authoritarian/ tribal societies, for example, acting on the belief that X is wrong because the chief or the tribal elders say it is). Celebrity endorsements of products make an implicit appeal to authority. (Celebrity A enjoys a particular brand of breakfast cereal, therefore, it is implied, so should you!)

In the given example, some may think that Plato's views on such matters are credible not just because he is a famous name, however, but because he thought long and hard and wrote extensive works about them.

For this reason, the term expertise is sometimes used. In general terms, appeals to expertise are more legitimate than appeals to authority, since expertise in a given field increases CREDIBILITY in a way that mere authority does not. Clearly the judgement here needs to be to what extent the expertise of the source is relevant to the view point he or she has been accredited with (an expert on stamp collecting has no obvious expertise when giving his or her viewpoint on acupuncture; see also, section on STATISTICAL REASONING for the example of how an expert in 'cot death' was evidently not an expert in statistics). There is also the issue of the extent to which someone can actually be an 'expert' in a given field (does being a professor of moral philosophy mean that a person's own moral beliefs are more likely to be correct? Can anyone, for example, Plato, have relevant knowledge about whether or not slavery is right or wrong?) Moreover, credibility is not the same as truth; therefore to assume that because an expert's view is credible it must be true, or we should therefore believe them, is to be guilty of an appeal to expertise.

Appeal to emotion/pity/anger/fear etc.

a technique used to persuade an audience of the truth or correctness of a viewpoint by relying upon an attempt to alter the audience's emotions.

Of all the APPEALS, this is usually considered the most 'unfair'/ illegitimate means of persuasion and yet one of the most commonly deployed. The group term, which applies to all, is an appeal to emotion; a more exact account of the particular emotion appealed to can be given by labelling the appeal as an 'appeal to fear' or 'appeal to pity'. The following appeal to emotion makes use of appeals to fear, anger, shame and pity:

> The future of the planet is in our hands. If we do not act now, today, then we are facing the prospect of almost certain devastation. Not to act is stupid, cowardly, lazy and selfish. We are racing towards catastrophe; our grandchildren's hopes depend on us.

Since the purpose of arguments is to persuade, it is natural for those engaging in argument, especially where they feel strongly about the matter at hand, to reach for PERSUASIVE LANGUAGE, which is often emotively charged. The effect is often such that an argument can appear a lot stronger (and hence be more persuasive) than it really is when the emotive element is removed:

> What happens in the future depends on what we do now. Not acting right away will lead to a high chance of something going quite badly wrong. It is also the wrong thing to do. It will have consequences for our grandchildren.

Although there may be a slight loss of meaning in translation, what has largely been lost is the emotional content, with the consequence that the argument seems a lot blander. The first version is far more likely to incite someone into acting, and thus is in effect more persuasive, even if no reasons exist in the first one that are not also in the second.

It is unlikely that in any given argument an appeal to emotion will replace rational support altogether. But the more the argument relies on this appeal, the weaker it is as an argument. Sometimes when people try to persuade they forsake argument in favour of appealing to people's emotions. This method of persuasion is commonly used in advertising or marketing (e.g. by appealing to people's sense of pride, shame, envy or fear), and is certainly the driving force behind much propaganda. By engaging and manipulating the emotions of the audience, the audience can be led to a viewpoint without having been provided with good or – in some cases any – rational support.

There is no reason why emotive language cannot be used in an argument. A key Critical Thinking skill, however, is to be able to extract the rational grounds being offered from the manner with which they are presented. The extent to which an argument is guilty of appealing to emotion depends to what extent it is judged that the reasoning depends on the emotional charge. If once the emotional element is removed the argument is severely weakened or collapses, then the argument is likely to be resting on such an appeal. An element of persuasive language chosen to emphasize reasons which are already strong is acceptable; when it is in the place of reasons, or to make the reasons seem much stronger than they in fact are, then the argument is said to rest on an appeal to emotion.

See also: RHETORICAL LANGUAGE.

Appeal to history/precedent

an attempt to support or justify a claim, or further strengthen an argument, on the grounds that something similar has (or perhaps has not) happened before.

> There is no chance of the English team winning this test match. No side has ever scored more than 450 runs to win a match in the last innings, and England needs 475.

The above argument could be said to be making an appeal to history. It may be that it is difficult, even impossible, for the England team to score the required runs, but that is not *because* (causally speaking) other teams have failed to score similar number of runs in similar conditions.

Here is an argument which makes an appeal to precedent:

> It might be possible for the England team to win this match. It's happened once before that a team batting last have managed to score 448 runs to win a match: Australia managed this, in the West Indies, in 1958.

As with all other appeals, the legitimacy of the appeal depends on the circumstances; in some cases the event (or events) in the past that is referred to may be of significant similarity for it to offer a degree of support for the viewpoint in question. Also, the frequency or regularity with which something has happened in the past will affect the confidence in the prediction that it will happen again (to argue that the car someone has bought is likely to break down because you know someone who had a similar model that used to break down is clearly a poor argument using an over-GENERALIZATION and therefore also making an unfair appeal to history/ precedent).

As a general rule, however, the fact that something has happened in the past does not mean that it will happen again; therefore the support will only ever be limited at best. Moreover, whether or not something has happened, has happened frequently, or will happen again, does not make it *right* that it should happen (see, APPEAL TO TRADITION).

Note that an appeal to history/ precedent can be seen as a form of ARGUMENT FROM ANALOGY. Judging the relevance or degree of support given by the appeal is similar to judging the effectiveness of an analogy, through considering the relevant similarities or differences between the event or events in the past and the current situation. As with an analogy, however similar the two things seem, the fact of precedent does not prove that the same thing will happen again; even good/ fair appeals to history/precedent will not offer conclusive support for their conclusions.

See also: APPEALS (GENERAL).

Appeal to popularity

a persuasive tactic, usually unfair, that argues or implies that since a view is widely held it ought to be accepted.

The truth of a claim is logically independent of the number of people who hold it. Take conspiracy theories. If it was revealed in a poll that the number of people who believed a particular conspiracy had risen markedly in recent months, would that in itself give reason to believe that the conspiracy was therefore more likely to be true?

The answer is no. False beliefs can be widespread (belief in any conspiracy theory indeed PRESUPPOSES this). If just one person happened to know the truth about a conspiracy theory and they kept it to him or her self that would not make it any less true than another theory that was popularly held but false.

Despite this, it is a fact of human nature that people's thoughts and behaviour are swayed by the thoughts and behaviour of others; hence the common tactic to include in arguments some reference to the fact that other people agree with the arguer's viewpoint ('It is commonly accepted that. . .'). The following argument makes use of an unfair appeal to popularity:

> A recent survey suggested that most people are unhappy with the speed of their broadband internet connection, believing that they are not being provided with the speed of service they had been promised. Clearly internet service providers are failing to meet the standards they advertise in their promotional literature.

The fact that people think or believe something does not make it so. Here the conclusion, that internet service providers are failing to meet the standards they advertise in their promotional literature, is not justified by the reason given, since the fact alone that people think their service is slower than it is supposed to be does not mean that it is; and the argument is therefore flawed (the inference to the conclusion a NON SEQUITUR). Another way to express this is that the reason is not relevant to the conclusion; some might say a reason has not even really been given (see, APPEALS and the view that they are better termed as rhetorical devices rather than flaws).

The relevance of what people think or believe in terms of justifying a claim can vary. For example, if it was common knowledge that there was an easy way of testing or determining the speed of your internet connection (perhaps by going to a well-known website that was able to do this reliably), then the fact that the majority of people believed that their connection speed was too slow would become more relevant. However, it would need this additional information, together with the ASSUMPTION that most people have bothered to check their speed in this way, for the reason to provide relevant rational support; without any of this, the reason provides no real JUSTIFICATION for the conclusion, and the appeal remains unfair.

As with all appeals, there are cases where the appeal alone is, at least potentially, relevant. In some cases, what people think *will* affect the truth of the claim. To take an obvious example, if the claim being argued for is one about the general mood or view of a nation or society, and the evidence cited is a poll in a paper which indicates that such a view is widely held, then this support is relevant. However, if this cited evidence is then used to argue that what they think is 'right' or 'true', then the appeal becomes fallacious. Consider the following examples:

- Polls indicate that public support for the Prime Minister has grown considerably in recent months. This shows that he is the right man for the job and ought to be given the opportunity to remain in power.
- Polls indicate that public support for the Prime Minister has grown considerably in recent months. This shows that he may still hold onto power in the forthcoming elections.

Clearly, the second argument (only) uses an appeal to popularity in a way which provides clear and relevant support for its conclusion.

A final note about appeals to popularity. Often the appeal is not used as a reason for a conclusion, but as a way of giving an otherwise unsupported reason (or assumption) the semblance of truth. Phrases such as 'Everyone agrees that', or 'It is commonly accepted that' are often used to introduce claims that are by no means certain, to establish them as grounds for an argument:

> It is commonly accepted amongst civilised nations that individuals ought to be free to express their opinions whatever the offence this may cause others. For this reason, the author has every right to say what he has said, and for the publishers to continue with the widespread publication and distribution of his work. . .

Here the unfair appeal to popularity is not used to give 'support' for a conclusion, but to make the original claim appear to be true or uncontroversial – when this is far from the case. (In this argument, there is no problem with the inference from the reason to the conclusion – if the reason is true, it gives very good grounds for the conclusion!) As always in Critical Thinking, the key is to consider how plausible or credible the claim is, or how solid the reasoning is, once shorn of the accompanying RHETORIC.

Appeal to tradition

an attempt to justify, or give the semblance of justification to, an attitude or course of action, on the grounds that such an attitude has always been the case, or has been the case for a significant matter of time.

An appeal to tradition is very similar to the appeal to history/precedent, and the terms can often be interchangeable. An appeal to tradition is usually made in an effort to justify the view that something that happens now is (morally/ socially) *acceptable*, whereas an appeal to history is used to support, or imply support, that something that has happened before will or won't happen again:

> Who says that prostitution is necessarily wrong, or that it should necessarily be illegal? After all, it's the oldest profession!

This is an argument that is often used in defence of prostitution. However, the fact that something has always been the case or has existed for a long time does not mean that it should be the case, or should continue to exist. (Other obvious examples would be phenomena such as slavery, rights of women and so forth.)

Compare the following, which is more accurately termed an appeal to history:

> Prostitution has always existed; therefore making it illegal is unlikely to prevent it.

In the above examples, the appeal to history provides better support for the claim it is trying to establish (and has less reason to be termed unfair), than the appeal to tradition. As with all the appeals, it is a matter of context, interpretation and judgement.

See also: APPEALS (GENERAL).

Argument

*a form of discourse which exists primarily to persuade, by giving reasons for
beliefs or claims; a complex expression consisting of one or more reasons and
a conclusion.*

It does not follow from the definition that any persuasive device, or any reason for acting or for believing something can be deemed an argument. An
argument is just one way among many to bring people to accept certain
views and/or reject others. A powerful image, or story, or offer of money or
threat may on occasions induce someone to adopt a certain position or make
a particular decision. But it is very questionable whether any of them can be
called 'arguments' other than metaphorically. We must also be careful not
to equate argument with RHETORICAL or emotive language. They are routinely
found in the texts we call arguments, but they are not arguments themselves.
In Critical Thinking, students have to be able to identify the *rational* argument
in a text, or the underlying argument, as distinct from any accompanying
rhetoric.

Another way in which argument is often defined is by identifying it with
REASONING. For example, it is said that human reasoning 'finds expression' in
argument, or that argument is the form of reasoning, or that a particular
argument *is* a piece of reasoning or a line of reasoning.

But reasoning, like persuasion, is a broader domain than argument. It includes
activities such as problem solving, decision making, questioning, explaining
and the like, which involve rational thinking but not necessarily in the form of
an argument. Moreover, there are forms of argument, in its broadest sense,
which have little or nothing to do with reasoning – for example, the mere
activity of disputing or quarrelling. So, although 'reasoning' and 'argument'
can be, and often are, used to refer to the same activity, or the same kind of
discourse, they are by no means synonymous.

Although we cannot use reasoning as a ready-made definition of argument, we can make useful references to the overlap between reasoning
and argument. For example, we can talk about a kind of reasoning *found
in* an argument – otherwise known as INFERENCE. Associating argument with

inference has some practical advantages, for example, when it comes to identifying and analysing samples of natural-language argument. Natural language contains words and phrases which frequently indicate inference namely 'therefore', 'so', 'because' and the like. This is a clue to the presence of reasoned argument. Naturally, not every natural-language argument contains an explicit inference indicator. However, if a text under consideration *is* an argument, one of these words can usually be inserted without altering the sense. For example:

> These banknotes are forgeries. They all have the same serial number. If they were genuine they would have different numbers.

Clearly we could replace the first full stop with 'because' thus indicating that the second and third sentences could be given as reasons to support the first sentence. It is a useful test, but it comes with a warning; most of the connectives which are used to indicate inference have other meanings and functions as well. 'Because' in particular is as much at home in explanations as it is in arguments, if not more so, and explanations are easy to confuse with arguments. (See, entry on ARGUMENT VERSUS EXPLANATION.)

Another approach to defining argument can be made by identifying its *formal* properties. This is often referred to as the standard definition, or the standard model or standard form of argument. A standard argument must have:

- a recognizable *conclusion*
- one or more *reasons* (or premises) offered in *support* of the conclusion.

This can be abbreviated to, for example:

R / C

Or:

$R_1, R_2, \ldots, R_n$ / C

with 'R' standing for a reason (or PREMISE), 'C' for a conclusion and a suitable separator (e.g. '/') for the relation of (purportedly) *following from* or *being supported by*.

This provides us with a strict definition to the effect that arguments are just those texts which conform to this model, or which can be plausibly reconstructed to conform to it, a procedure that is common practice in Critical Thinking and informal logic:

R$_1$: If these banknotes were genuine they would have different serial numbers.

R$_2$: These banknotes all have the same serial number.

-------------Therefore---------------

C: These banknotes are forgeries.

Two conditions must be met. First, that this reconstruction really does preserve the meaning of the original text and second that it makes good sense to say that *if* R$_1$ and R$_2$ are true then C follows; or – which is the same thing – that R$_1$ and R$_2$ support or give grounds for asserting C.

The model given here is of a simple argument. However, the term 'argument' can also be used to mean complex structures with intermediate conclusions and sub-arguments. (See, ARGUMENT STRUCTURE.)

Although the standard model is useful in providing a method for analysing argument, and for testing samples to see if they conform, it begs the question somewhat as a definition. It relies on the meaning of expressions such as 'conclusion' and 'following from. . .'. Yet to understand such terms we already need to have an idea of what goes on in a reasoned argument. It is the concepts and practice of argument, reasoning, inference and such like, which give meaning to these terms, not the other way round.

The other problem with a purely structural definition is that many natural-language arguments are difficult to fit into the mould. Many are elliptical, for example, with missing or unstated premises (see, ASSUMPTION) or have implicit rather than stated conclusions, often leaving room for conflicting interpretations. What are we to make of, for instance:

Oh come on. Look at the evidence. The ice is melting, right?

Clearly this is argumentative. Its tone is evidently persuasive. Do we say that fragments like this are variant arguments or quasi-arguments? Or do we say they are not arguments at all, given the formal definition that stipulates 'R . . . (therefore) C' as a minimum requirement?

Summary

The purpose of this entry is to show that argument does not have a single, all-purpose definition. In Critical Thinking the concept of argument should be explored very thoroughly, and its boundaries discussed; but it is counter-productive to expect to pin it down to a rigid set of conditions or paradigms. Context is crucial too. There is no one *kind* of argument as it is used in logic, debating, journalism, or science, or in day-to-day decision making and so on. Nor is any one of them the right or predominant one. Where Critical Thinking differs from classical logic is that it has to grapple with arguments from all these contexts and more, and come up with an effective *modus operandi* for dealing with the diversity.

That said, the following can be thought of as contributing to an understanding of 'argument', as the term is most commonly used in Critical Thinking:

- Argument is a tool for *persuasion.*
- Argument is the form much *reasoning* takes.
- An argument is a set of (one or more) claims offered in *support* of a further claim.
- An argument is a way of expressing *inference.*
- Arguments are texts in which there is a high incidence of the words 'therefore', 'so', 'because'. . . etc.
- Arguments are constructions with the form 'Reason/s (therefore) Conclusion'; or complex chains of such arguments.

See also: REASONING, INFERENCE, ARGUMENT INDICATOR and ARGUMENT STRUCTURE.

Argument indicator

words or phrases which signal the presence of argument in natural language by connecting reasons and conclusions. They are also known as INFERENCE *indicators (or, more technically, as* illatives*). The most familiar examples are*: 'therefore', 'so' and 'because'.

These banknotes have the same serial numbers, *so* they must be forgeries.

There are two main classes of argument indicators, depending on whether they attach to the conclusion of an argument, or to one of the reasons (premises). They can be thought of as *therefore-type*, or *because-type* indicators respectively.

Conclusion indicators (therefore-type): {therefore, so, thus, hence, consequently, for which reason, from which it follows that, as a result. . .}

Reason indicators (because-type): {because, since, as, on account of, given that. . .}

Note that many expressions which function as argument indicators may also function as EXPLANATION indicators. For instance:

I won't accept these banknotes because they are forgeries.

Here the reason, 'they are forgeries', is not given to *argue that* I won't accept the banknotes, but to *explain why* I won't.

There is another class of expressions which provide clues to the presence of reasoning but which are not connectives. What they indicate are kinds of assertion for which argument is commonly needed – for example, recommendations, advice, proposals, normative claims etc. Take the claim:

The government *needs to* do more to crack down on forgery. It is becoming a serious drain on the economy.

The marker for the recommendation (to crack down on forgery) is the phrase 'needs to'. ('Must', 'should', 'ought to' etc. would have done just as well.) Such indicators not only help to identify argument but also to identify the conclusion within an argument.

See also: ARGUMENT and ARGUMENT VERSUS EXPLANATION.

Argument structure

the way in which the constituent parts of an argument are organized or related.

The basic structure of a simple argument is:

R / C or R, R, R. . .; C

where 'C' represents the conclusion and 'R' the reason or reasons (premises, grounds) that are offered to support 'C'. The separator (/ or) is equivalent to the English word 'therefore'. (See, ARGUMENT INDICATOR.) In natural-language texts, the order in which these parts appear may vary, and the actual connective used may vary too, or be omitted.

For example:

Boxing should be banned. No sport should be permitted in which the object is to inflict injury. Boxers purposely set out to injure one another.

This passage can be understood as a simple argument, and its structure can be revealed by analysis, that is, by reconstructing the original text according to the standard form above:

R1: No sport should be permitted in which the object is to inflict injury.

R2: Boxers purposely set out to injure one another.

-----------------------------Therefore---------------------------------

C: Boxing should be banned.

In this reconstruction we can see that the two reasons R1 and R2 combine to support C. Note that R1 and R2 are interdependent; each needs the other to give adequate grounds for the argument. Another way to express this is that the reasons are needed jointly. In some Critical Thinking textbooks this structure is called JOINT REASONING. In this example, both R1 and R2 are needed to support the conclusion. If R2 were false, R1 would not be an adequate reason to ban boxing. Indeed, it would not be a reason at all. Likewise if R2 were false R1 would not be a reason. This structure can be shown in a diagram linking R1 and R2 to the conclusion by a single arrow:

R1   R2
$\downarrow$
C

Not all reasons combine in this way; some are independent of each other. Suppose, for example, we were to supplement the argument with another premise:

R3: Boxing is a corrupt sport which attracts crime.

This claim could be brought into the argument. If R3 were true – which it may or may not be – it would add extra support, that is, support from a different angle. It would therefore have a separate arrow in the diagram:

R1   R2
$\downarrow$ $\swarrow$R3
C

We now have two lines of reasoning pointing to C, one from the perspective of injury and the other from the perspective of corruption and crime. This strengthens the argument because if either R1 or R2 were challenged, there is still R3 as a reason for C.

Complex structures

Another way to strengthen an argument is to provide support for the *reasons*. For example, what are the grounds for claiming R1? Who *says* no such sport should be permitted? Anticipating this objection, the author might choose to provide a separate, sub-argument to support R1:

In all civilised societies there are laws prohibiting assault. Sport is no exception, or at least it shouldn't be. Therefore no sport should be permitted in which the object is to inflict injury.

In this argument the claim we called 'R1' is now the conclusion, with its own supporting reasons. If we want to combine the two lines of reasoning to form one argument, we need to relabel the parts. There are various ways to do it. Here is one:

R1: In all civilised societies there are laws prohibiting assault.

R2: Sport is no exception. . .

\---

C1: No sport should be permitted in which the object is to inflict injury.

R3: Boxers purposely set out to injure each other.

R4: Boxing is a corrupt sport which attracts crime.

\---

C2: Boxing should be banned.

This is a complex argument as it has two conclusions. First there is a sub-argument in which R1 and R2 combine to support C1. C1 and R3 then combine to support C2, with additional support from R4. In diagram form:

C1 can also be called the INTERMEDIATE CONCLUSION (IC for short), and C2 the main conclusion. The exact wording is largely a matter of preference. Indeed, there is no one 'correct' format or method for analysing argument. It can be done in words or in symbols or in diagrams, so long as the structure is clearly revealed and matches the sense of the original text.

See also: ARGUMENT and CHAIN OF REASONING.

Argument (inference) to the best explanation

See: ABDUCTION.

Argument versus explanation

Arguments and explanations are easily mistaken for one another. Grammatically, they are practically indistinguishable, and share many of the same connectives, namely, 'because', 'since', 'therefore' and the like. This is not surprising since both arguments and explanations give REASONS. However, the reasons in an argument and the reasons in an explanation are not of the same kind.

The reasons in an *argument* are reasons to accept or believe a claim which, without the argument, might be disputed or questioned or disbelieved. The argument may not persuade someone to believe or agree with the claim, but that it is what it is supposed to do. For example:

> The Minister should be forced to resign immediately *because* he has accepted illegal donations.

Or:

> The Minister has accepted illegal donations *so* he should be forced to resign.

Here the reason – that the Minister has accepted illegal donations – is given as grounds for a recommendation that the Minister should be made to resign. In other words, it is inferred or concluded from the claim that the Minister accepted the illegal donations.

Compare this with:

> The Minister has announced his resignation because he had accepted illegal donations.

Here the first part of the sentence is presented as a fact. It is not being inferred from the second sentence, nor is the author attempting to persuade anyone that it is right; it is presumed to be true, and the reason that is given for it is purely explanatory. 'It *accounts* for his resignation' is another way to put it.

This means that explanations do not have conclusions, whereas arguments do. We could say that the announcing of the resignation by the minister is the *result* or *consequence of* the taking of donations, but not the *'conclusion from. . .'.*

The technical terms, if they are required, are:

- *explanandum*: what is being explained
- *explanans*: the explanatory claim(s), the reason(s).

Assertion

CLAIM *or statement.*

An assertion is a speech act in which a claim or statement is made. Although it sometimes carries the extra connotation of being a forceful expression, in Critical Thinking 'assertion' and CLAIM are used more or less interchangeably.

Assessment

summative judgement, for example, of an argument or other text.

In Critical Thinking 'assessment' is often an alternative term for EVALUATION, that is, judging the quality, effectiveness, soundness etc. of a piece of reasoning. It can also be used to mean a combination of ANALYSIS *and* evaluation, in which case it is more inclusive than 'evaluation' alone. When giving students an instruction to assess or critically assess an argument, it should be made clear which of these two senses is intended.

Assumption

an unsupported claim or belief that has been taken for granted as being true.

In philosophical logic, an assumption is something that is as yet unproved. Since an argument has to begin somewhere, statements have to be given that are not themselves justified in the argument. For this reason, logicians and often philosophers refer to premises as 'assumptions'. In Critical Thinking the more everyday term 'reason' is preferred.

In its everyday sense, an assumption is a claim that has been taken for granted, yet the truth of which is not commonly accepted. For example, if someone said of a man on trial 'He's clearly innocent; therefore he ought not to be punished/ convicted', the first claim would rightly be termed an 'assumption'. The second claim is supported by the first, so it itself is not an assumption, even though it relies on one.

This everyday sense is much closer to the way the term is used in Critical Thinking. It is similar in this sense to 'claim', yet with a greater degree of implied scepticism. However, the most important difference between the word 'claim' and 'assumption' is that a claim is always something that has been stated. An assumption, however, may refer to a belief that someone holds in their mind which has not been expressed publicly in language.

What has made the term tricky is that it has often come to mean an implicit assumption; in other words, something that has not been stated but its truth has been assumed nonetheless. In the above example, it has not been stated that 'innocent people should not be convicted/ punished'; yet this belief needs to be accepted for the argument to work and the conclusion to follow. This kind of assumption may or may not be conscious. Either way, the argument still makes this assumption, and therefore we can say that the arguer has 'assumed that innocent people should not be punished' even though they have not stated so.

These kinds of assumptions that we make in our thinking are linked to our *cognitive biases* (a big area in the psychology of Critical Thinking, which looks at the way that different people often interpret the same or very similar information differently, or draw different conclusions according to the background, beliefs or expectations of which they have little conscious awareness). A great virtue of becoming skilled at Critical Thinking is that, through learning to spot where implicit assumptions are being made (either by yourself or someone else), you can learn to detect cognitive biases and to question them, or challenge them, if necessary.

There is a debate sometimes about whether or not an assumption can be a flaw in an argument. Strictly, speaking, each of the informal fallacies can be interpreted as an UNWARRANTED ASSUMPTION that the arguer has made. For example, an argument that commits the post hoc fallacy is *assuming* that because something happened before something else it must have been the cause; likewise the flaw of generalization if the arguer *assumes* that the particular examples they have cited indicate a general law. If, as is likely, these assumptions are unwarranted, then the argument is evidently flawed.

See also: CLAIM, ASSERTION and UNWARRANTED ASSUMPTION.

Begging the question

assuming, explicitly or implicitly, what you are arguing for.

'Begging the question' is a rough and rather antiquated translation of the Latin *petitio principii*. This literally means 'request for the beginning' (*principium*), which is even less illuminating. What begging the question means in practical terms is assuming, or helping oneself to the very claim that is being debated, at issue or in question. It is in that sense that 'question' should be understood.

Suppose, for example, I want to argue against the 'right to roam' act, which allows the public free access to the open countryside even if it is privately owned. My argument might take the following form:

> A landowner has an absolute right to choose whether or not to permit the public access to his or her private property. Without such permission the public are trespassing, which no one is or should be entitled to do. Therefore the public has no right to roam.

Clearly I am begging the question. The long-running debate to which this argument belongs centres precisely on the question of how far a landowner's rights extend with respect to public access; or, conversely, to what extent the public have a natural right to wander freely. My opening premise simply *closes* the debate in my favour but without any supporting reason or justification. If the landowner does have an absolute right, as the above argument claims, then a public right to roam is more or less a contradiction.

Notice, too, the RHETORICAL LANGUAGE which emphasizes the question-begging nature of the argument, namely, 'absolute', 'private property' and especially 'trespassing'. Trespassing is illegal, so to say that someone is trespassing automatically implies that they are in the wrong. Again, I am assuming exactly what I am arguing for.

Who *says* that landowners have this 'absolute right'? Well, opponents of the right to roam act do, if they adopt the line of reasoning given above.

The problem they face is that their argument can be pre-empted by anyone who reasons instead that the *public* has an absolute right to countryside access, and/or that any landowner who declares his or her land private is infringing that right. Of course, they too are begging the question unless they can show by further reasoning that the public right supersedes the landowners' rights.

Arguments which blatantly beg the question are generally regarded as fallacious. Indeed, begging the question is one of the 'classic fallacies'. They are often described as CIRCULAR. An argument is fully circular if its conclusion is effectively a restatement of one or more of its supporting premises. For example:

> Trespass is wrong and that is why there is a law against it. It is wrong to do anything illegal. Therefore it is wrong to trespass.

Finally, it is worth noting that people often misuse the phrase 'begging the question' to mean 'raising the question'. Consider:

> A study, published recently in the Lancet, has found that sufferers of chronic fatigue syndrome ('ME') are more likely to recover if receive Cognitive Behaviour Therapy and they are helped to do more exercise than they think they can. This begs the question whether chronic fatigue syndrome is a psychological disease afterall, and not a physical disease as some groups claim.

In this passage, there is no assumption of the initial point of claim under debate; 'begs the question' in this text simply means 'raises the question' and, as such, represents a non-technical and misuse of the term.

See: CIRCULARITY.

Bias

an inclination to give greater weight to one particular viewpoint on an issue when more than one viewpoint is possible.

Bias needs to be distinguished from firmly held views that have been arrived at by rational consideration of evidence and arguments. Persons, arguments and documents can all be described as biased, that is, as giving greater weight to an opinion or conclusion than the evidence for it warrants.

In relation to persons, the word 'bias' is used by Critical Thinking in the everyday sense of an attitude of mind in favour of or against one particular viewpoint or one particular side of a dispute. Individuals are not always aware of bias in their own judgements.

In arguments and documents, bias may be identifiable by the use of emotive language, selective use of evidence and apparently unwarranted assumptions.

A biased opinion is not necessarily false, but it has been arrived at without the appropriate critical consideration.

See also: PREJUDICE.

Causal explanation

an explanation of an event or phenomenon in terms of what caused it.

For example, if gale force winds have brought down some power cables, and a town's electrical supply has failed as a result, we can say that the high wind *caused* the power failure, or that the power failure was an *effect* of the high winds, along with other effects, perhaps, such as damage to buildings. Alternatively we can say that the high winds explain the power failure. These accounts are two sides of the same coin.

However, in the context of Critical Thinking care must be taken not to *infer* a causal explanation from the mere concurrence of events. For example, if I have simply witnessed the gale and on the same day I experience a power failure, it cannot be assumed that there is any causal connection. It might be a *plausible* explanation. It might even be the best explanation available, in which case it would be reasonable to believe, or entertain the hypothesis, that the wind was the cause. But so long as there are other *possible* explanations – for example, a strike by workers at the power station – the inference is less than 100 per cent safe.

Nevertheless, it is common in much scientific reasoning for a causal explanation to be the conclusion of an argument. A doctor, for example, might reason from a set of familiar symptoms in a patient, that their cause (or causal explanation) is a certain medical condition – for example, flu. Although this may not be conclusive grounds for the diagnosis, it will still be a good argument if, in the doctor's experience, the symptoms and the condition always, or at least usually, coincide. Although it would be wrong to conclude that the symptoms could not *possibly* have any other cause, we would still want to say that the argument was a good one, if as a rule it results in good medical practice.

Cause and effect

See: CAUSAL EXPLANATION.

Certainty

absence of doubt; complete assurance; a claim whose truth is unquestionable.

In his *Naturalis Historia* Pliny the Elder (23–76 AD), wrote that the only certainty we can have is that nothing is certain! Many philosophers, scientists and others have echoed this saying, and taken it seriously for if we approach claims to knowledge with a completely open mind, everything that we believe may be subject to some doubt. As Descartes observed, even the evidence of our senses could be a delusion created by an evil demon. Unlikely? Yes, but impossible? No.

We find grounds for Pliny's remark, too, in the history of science. It is well recognized that the most firmly held scientific theories of one generation can be modified or even overturned in a later generation. To give the classic example, the earth's position at the centre of the universe had for most people the status of a certainty until the Copernican revolution. Now we are equally convinced that the earth is one ordinary planet among many orbiting the sun. Are the 'certainties' we claim today any more immune to revision than those of the past?

The strictest definition of 'certainty' can be found in mathematics, where certainty represents one extreme on a scale of PROBABILITY. Numerically probability is measured from 0 to 1, 0 being 'impossible', 1 being 'certain'. If we have a claim that we consider 'as likely as not' to be true, we would rate its probability as 0.5. Anything above that would be true 'on the balance of probabilities'. For a claim that comes close to certainty, or is 'beyond reasonable doubt,' we would expect a rating just below, but never quite, 1.

Consider the prediction that if I buy one lottery ticket I will *not* win the jackpot in the next national lottery draw. The probability of this being true is approximately 0.9999993, but despite this minute margin, no one would say it was certain, or that winning was impossible. We might even withhold saying that it was beyond reasonable doubt, since every week or so one or more people do win the lottery. Not only *could* it happen, it *does*.

In Critical Thinking the concept of certainty is relevant in connection with our evaluation of claims to knowledge. Strictly speaking knowledge requires certainty, since we cannot really claim to *know* something that may be false. However, there are few if any claims that can be made with certainty of the kind discussed above. An extreme SCEPTIC might conclude from this that there is or can be no such thing as knowledge, and some do; but extreme scepticism is not in keeping with Critical Thinking, where the aim is to make reasoned judgements using ordinary, everyday reasoning, not to demand a cast-iron proof for every claim encountered.

It is appropriate, therefore, to make a distinction between *absolute* certainty and *practical* certainty. Practical certainty is what we require of ordinary FACTS, such as well-documented observations, reliable inferences and convincing explanations. It is a fact of this kind that water freezes below 0°C, or that an egg will break if dropped on to a concrete floor from shoulder height, or that bees carry pollen or that reptiles are cold-blooded. Yes, the laws of nature could *conceivably* change overnight and turn these facts into falsehoods, but in the meantime they are as close to certainties as it is possible to get.

See also: FACT AND OPINION, JUSTIFICATION, PROBABILITY and SCEPTICISM.

Chain of reasoning

a sequence of connected arguments.

These chains occur when two or more simple arguments are linked to form a longer, complex argument. Each argument has its own conclusion which then becomes a reason (or premise) for a further argument.

For example:

> The recession is going to make it harder for the company to borrow capital. Therefore savings will have to be made instead. Therefore staffing cuts are going to be unavoidable. Therefore in fairness employees ought to be warned now so that they know what to expect.

(This is a rather unnatural, artificial-sounding example because of all the uses of 'therefore'. They have been put in to emphasize the idea of a chain.)

It is not only whole arguments that can be formed into chains of reasoning. Here is a chain of hypothetical (conditional) claims leading to a conclusion:

> If you get tired you are likely to start making mistakes. If you make mistakes then you endanger other members of the team. If one of your team-mates

gets hurt because of your mistake you will never forgive yourself. Therefore you should take regular rest-breaks.

Although this is a single argument, it is legitimate to call this a chain of reasoning, as each hypothetical claim has been reached by a process of causal reasoning.

See also: ARGUMENT STRUCTURE and COMPLEX ARGUMENT.

Circularity and circular reasoning

restatement without saying anything new; using the conclusion of an argu-ment as a reason.

A simple example of circularity can be found in definitions. For example, if a dictionary were to define a *ball* as 'a spherical object', and elsewhere define *spherical* as 'ball-shaped', it would be guilty of circularity. In a sense all dic-tionary-style definitions are ultimately circular (though usually less obviously) because they consist of synonyms – words and phrases which mean the same as each other. They are useful only to someone who already knows the mean-ing of one of the terms, for instance, if I know what a ball is but not what a sphere is. If I know neither (or both), the definitions would tell me nothing.

We also find circularity in arguments. Suppose, for example, I told someone that it was wrong to work on the Sabbath, and when asked why I replied 'Because that's the one day of the week when people should refrain from work'. Clearly this argument is circular because it gives no *independent* reason for not working on the Sabbath. The reason merely restates the conclusion, or the conclusion restates the reason, whichever way you want to look at it. Circular reasoning is generally regarded as at best weak and at worst falla-cious. When deemed fallacious it is sometimes described as 'viciously circular'. It is also referred to sometimes as BEGGING THE QUESTION.

See also: BEGGING THE QUESTION.

Claim

another word for statement.

A general term to describe any statement or assertion – whether fact or opinion. Grammatically a claim must be expressible in the form of a declarative sentence. Any sentence in the declarative mood will be making at least one claim. Since not all sentences are declarative ('Give me the money!' is issuing a command, not declaring anything to be the case), and since compound sentences can express several claims ('I like cricket, he likes football, and she likes rowing'), the word 'claim' is preferred. Moreover, unlike 'fact' or 'opinion' the word is (mostly) neutral, lacking the connotations that these words convey (see, FACT AND OPINION).

Claims *can* be implied through non-declarative sentences, the most obvious example being rhetorical questions, where the claim being implied is the unstated answer. The claim is not the question but the implied answer, which will be expressible in the form of a declarative sentence (See, RHETORICAL LANGUAGE).

Put simply a claim is a statement which purports to be true. A statement does not have to *be* true to be a claim. Someone can claim something that is false, for example, when people lie or are mistaken. But a claim is purporting, or proposing a statement that it is asserting to be the case.

Although the word 'claim' correctly describes any statement that purports to be true, it is most meaningfully applied to statements where the truth is (to some extent) still in doubt or at least not completely accepted. A simple statement of fact such as 'Mary was born in England' would be more cautiously called a claim if there was some question mark about the speaker's CREDIBILITY ('John claimed Mary was born in England'). While maintaining neutrality, the word 'claim' does also imply a distancing; it distances the author from acceding to the truth of the original statement. It implies an openness with regard to whether or not the statement is true. In certain contexts, and given certain intonations, it can convey something of the pejorative meaning that the word opinion carries, though much less so. (Person A: 'He said that it was true.' Person B (correcting): 'He *claimed* that it was true.')

A simple way of defining an argument is as a series of one or more claims, where one is supported by, or supposed to follow from, the others. As a critical thinker the aim is to respond critically, yet also fairly and objectively, to arguments. It is therefore helpful to think of the statements that

comprise arguments as being claims, as this encourages both a more critical, as well as a more objective approach to analysis and evaluation. Very
often the statements in arguments *are* best described as claims. Arguments,
in attempting to persuade others that there are good, rational grounds for
a belief, are seldom reliant on claims that are obviously mere opinion. At
the same time, they naturally go beyond the world of agreed fact (otherwise there would be no need to reach for an argument). Besides, unlike
the word 'assumption', the word 'claim' applies equally to reasons and
conclusions, as well as to statements giving evidence, counter-assertions
or background.

It is also a useful word to use outside the context of arguments, for example, 'What do you make of the opposition leader's claim that the military
are under-funded?' Using the word claim is less pejorative than the word
'opinion' or even the word 'assumption' (the claim may not have been an
assumption, but something that was supported by argument).

Since 'claim' is such a broad term, and therefore non-specific – hence non-
informative – it is often useful to specify the type of claim. Some important
examples are generalization, value judgement, (Statement of) Principle, conditional statement, hypothesis, prediction, recommendation, allegation and
definition.

See also: ASSERTION, ASSUMPTION, PROPOSITION, FACT AND OPINION and TRUTH.

Clarifying meaning

removing any ambiguities, vagueness or imprecision in language.

Clarifying meaning is an important process in CRITICAL THINKING, because we
cannot evaluate someone's REASONING if we do not fully understand it. The
need for clarification arises both when one is trying to assess someone else's
reasoning, and when one is attempting to present clear and precise reasoning
of one's own.

In the case of assessing reasoning, clarifying meaning involves:

- identifying the possible interpretations of any ambiguous or vague words or phrases
- trying to judge from the context which interpretation is intended
- considering the implications for the reasoning of the various possible interpretations, if it is unclear which interpretation is intended
- judging the quality of the reasoning or ARGUMENT in relation to each possible interpretation.

Here is an example of reasoning whose meaning is unclear in a number of places:

> There is a prevalent idea that because most body heat is lost through the head, we should always wear a hat when we go outside in cold weather. An article in the British Medical Journal disputes this, but a recent radio broadcast that tried to disprove it made a big mistake. The presenter sent two subjects to stand in the cold, one wearing a hat, and the other bareheaded. After a while the body temperatures of both subjects were taken, and were found to be the same. The presenter concluded that no heat had been lost by the person with the bare head. What he didn't realise is that we have a self-regulating system for body temperature, so that is why the temperatures were the same, and also why we don't need to wear a hat when we go out in cold weather.

What needs to be clarified?

- First 'most body heat is lost through the head' is ambiguous; it could mean 'most of the heat that the body generates is lost through the head' or 'most of the heat that the body loses is lost through the head'.
- If it means the latter, does it simply mean that people who don't wear hats lose more body heat through the head than those who do wear hats?
- Does the phrase 'an article in the British Medical Journal disputes this' mean the article disputes that most body heat is lost through the head, or that one should always wear a hat when outside in cold weather, or both?
- Finally, in explaining why the attempted proof was mistaken, the vague phrase 'self-regulating system for body temperature' is used. Given the claim that because of this we don't need to wear a hat, the author seems to

be claiming that the self-regulating system ensures that regardless of how much body heat is lost, the body can always maintain its temperature. But as an explanation of why the temperatures of the two subjects were the same, it only needs to be true that the body can regulate its temperature in most but not necessary all environmental conditions.

See also: AMBIGUITY, EQUIVOCATION and VAGUENESS.

Coherence

the property of a collection of beliefs or claims such that they fit together as a unified whole.

The basic idea behind the virtue of coherence is that of making sense, as in the phrase 'his speech was coherent' as opposed to mumbled, garbled and unintelligible. As such it is property not of single or isolated beliefs but of collections of beliefs or claims. To describe several beliefs or claims as coherent is to assert that they go together in such a way as to make perfect sense together as a whole.

For a group of claims to make sense together, to count as coherent, five conditions must be satisfied: (i) They must be free from CONTRADICTIONS. In other words, the set of beliefs must not contain both the claim that p and the claim that not p. (ii) They must be free from INCONSISTENCIES, that is, they must not contain beliefs or claims which though formally free from contradiction (does not contain both p and not p) do contain beliefs which together entail a contradiction. For example, the belief set made up of the following three beliefs:

1. Socrates is a philosopher.
2. All philosophers are women.
3. Socrates is not a woman.

does not contain a formal contradiction. None of the claims 1–3 stand to one another as contradictories. However, it is obvious that the belief set, 1–3 is formally INCONSISTENT. In other words, the set of beliefs entails the further belief or claim that:

4. Socrates is a woman.

Clearly belief 4 is entailed by the conjunction of 1 and 2. So although the belief set is free, as it stands, from a formal contradiction it entails a contradiction, in that it entails 4 which is the contradictory of 3. That means the set of beliefs is inconsistent though not contradictory.

Now coherence among beliefs or claims requires minimally that the beliefs or claims are both free from contradiction and free from inconsistency. But clearly these two necessary conditions are not sufficient for a set of beliefs to be counted as coherent. This can be seen by considering the following four common beliefs:

1. Dogs bark.
2. France is in Europe.
3. The nights are lighter in summer than in winter.
4. Grass is green.

These four claims are free from contradiction and free from inconsistency. They are not contradictories nor do they entail contradictories. But they do not as they stand possess the virtue of coherence. They do not form a unified whole. For a collection of beliefs to count as coherent three further conditions must be satisfied. These are: (iii) the beliefs or claims should be mutually supporting. They should stand to one another in relations of justification so that holding some of the beliefs makes the others more reasonable; (iv) ideally a coherent body of beliefs should be complete – there should be no gaps as unfinished work cannot be described as fully coherent; (v) the whole should be organized by overarching systematic principles which unify different areas together. A coherent body of beliefs should not be like a gerrymandered building with lots and lots of AD HOC additions placed side by side. Thus, it can be seen that the sciences approximate most closely today to the virtue of coherence for it is the sciences which aspire to build up complete, systematic and unified bodies of belief.

To sum up, a collection of beliefs or claims are judged to be coherent when they satisfy the following five conditions:

1. free from contradiction
2. free from inconsistency
3. mutually supporting

4. complete
5. systematic and principled.

Complex arguments

constructions which contain one or more sub-arguments, as well as the main argument.

Complex arguments contrast with simple arguments. Structurally a simple argument has a single conclusion and one or more supporting reasons. A complex argument, on the other hand, has one or more INTERMEDIATE (subsidiary) CONCLUSIONS leading, often with additional premises, to a final or main conclusion.

See also: ARGUMENT STRUCTURE.

Conclusion

a claim which is based on, or inferred from, one or more other claims known as premises or reasons.

In a simple, standard argument there is one conclusion for which the reasons directly offer support. In complex arguments there may be one or more sub-arguments, leading to intermediate conclusions, which in turn lead to a main conclusion.

It is not always possible, in non-standard arguments (or sub-arguments) to identify a single grammatical statement as the conclusion. It may be in the form of a rhetorical question or command. In longer texts the conclusion may be repeated more than once and in more than one form or it may be implied rather than stated. In such cases, when a conclusion cannot be identified verbatim in the text, it may be summarized or paraphrased or inferred from the context instead.

For example:

> People are constantly encouraged to save for their retirement so that they can afford the expensive care they may need when they are old. But why?

What's the point? Savings just wither away because of low returns on investments and rising inflation, and if you haven't got any savings when you need the care the state pays for it anyway.

In this text the conclusion, such as it is, is expressed by the questions, 'But why?' and 'What's the point?' If this is an argument, what it is saying is that it is questionable whether people should save for their retirement – or puzzling that they are encouraged to do so – on the grounds that savings wither away and the state pays for care anyway.

See also: ARGUMENT and ARGUMENT STRUCTURE.

Conditional statement

A two-part statement where one part is presented as a consequence of the other, usually expressed in the form 'If. . ., then. . .'.

Conditional statements are claims expressing a relationship between two claims, such that the truth of one claim is a consequence of the truth of the other. For example, the statement 'If you believe in free speech, then you can't complain if people say things you find offensive' expresses the relationship between believing in free speech and not complaining if people say things you find offensive. It is important to realize that the claim is not asserting that either the claim 'You believe in free speech' or 'You can't complain if people say things you find offensive' is true or false; merely that the relation between them is such that, if the first is true, then so is the second. Since the claim made is about the relation between two claims, it is not possible to split the claim; the claim is a (single) complex claim.

The usefulness of such a claim is that it does not commit the author to accept the truth of the first part (the antecedent); thereby it allows focus merely on its implications. It is therefore the basis of all HYPOTHETICAL REASONING; for example, *If* (the conclusion to your argument is true), *then* (X is also likely to be true).

Since the truth of a conditional claim depends on the relation between the two propositions, it is possible to have conditional statements that are true even if one or more of the constituent statements are false. For example, 'If Anthony is a bachelor, then he is not married' is true even if it is false that Anthony is a bachelor and that he is not married.

Conditional statements are not always expressed in the 'If. . ., then. . .' form. The 'then' is often omitted, and there are synonymous expressions, such as the subjunctive '*Should* it rain, play will have to stop'. Similarly, the order of the claims can be reversed; the claim that is logically antecedent can occur after the consequent, for instance, 'Play will have to stop, should it rain'. It is therefore more accurate to talk of the 'antecedent' and the 'consequent' than the 'first' or the 'second' part of the claim.

Sometimes the relationship is purely logical, or one of definition; for example, 'If he is married then he cannot be a bachelor'. More commonly the relationship is a causal one – 'If you work hard, then you will do well in your exams'. A common mistake is to confuse the implications of such an assertion: for example, it is a mistake to assume the CONVERSE is true; it is a mistake to argue, on the basis of the conditional statement, that since (or if) the consequent is true, then the antecedent is true too (i.e. to think that if someone has done well in their exams, then they must have worked hard). This commits the logical fallacy of affirming the consequent (see, FALLACY, FORMAL); it also confuses NECESSARY AND SUFFICIENT CONDITIONS.

For this reason, the term 'conditional' can be misleading. If the truth of the second claim is thought of as conditional on the truth of the first claim, this implies that the second claim is not true unless the first one is, which confuses necessary conditions with sufficient. It is better to think in terms of the second claim being consequent on the former.

The meaning of a conditional statement is very similar to that of a HYPOTHETICAL statement, and the two terms can often be applied correctly to describe a single claim. However, the scope of conditional statements is broader. A statement is hypothetical if and only if it presents a situation that is as yet unproved or imaginary. Therefore, all hypothetical claims are conditional, but not all conditional claims are hypothetical (see, HYPOTHETICAL REASONING).

See also: NECESSARY AND SUFFICIENT CONDITIONS and HYPOTHETICAL REASONING.

Conflation

the combination or confusion of two ideas or concepts.

The word 'conflation' has a specialized meaning in relation to literature, that is, a work of literature created by combining two or more texts. In this context the term does not have a negative connotation, as it usually does in Critical Thinking.

In Critical Thinking the term 'conflation' generally refers to treating two ideas or concepts as the same when it is at least questionable whether they are the same. For example, if someone argues that euthanasia should remain against the law on the grounds that murder is illegal, they may be accused of conflating euthanasia and murder, thereby suggesting that there is no difference between the two. Whether or not their reasoning should be judged to be flawed will depend upon whether they can present good reasons for accepting that the two are similar in relevant respects.

Conflation is regarded as an informal FALLACY in arguments in which two clearly distinct concepts are treated as synonymous to support the conclusion. This is evident in the following argument:

> How can it be wrong to lie to a child about the identity of its father? Sometimes this is done because the adult thinks it would be best for the child, and, in any case, there is no law against telling a lie.

Here a major reason for the implied conclusion that it is not wrong (i.e. not morally wrong) to lie to a child is that there is no law against telling a lie. The confusion is between what is legal and what is moral, or between the concepts of legality and morality. It could be said that this example also involves the fallacy of EQUIVOCATION, since it is reasonable to assume that in the conclusion 'wrong' means 'morally wrong', whereas the reason assumes that 'wrong' means simply 'against the law'. However, the equivocation arises from the conflation of legality and morality.

Both equivocation and conflation involve misuse (accidental or deliberate) of language; equivocation treats an ambiguous term as if it had only one meaning and conflation treats terms with different meanings as if they were synonymous.

See also: AMBIGUITY.

Consistency

a property of two or more claims such that both or all could be true at the same time.

For example, the following two claims are consistent with each other, because both can be true at the same time:

1. Scotland generally has colder winters than England.
2. Scotland has a greater percentage of mountainous terrain than England.

Claim 1 is inconsistent with a claim that in most winters England is colder than Scotland; claim 2 is inconsistent with a claim that England is a more mountainous country than Scotland. To say that claims are consistent is not to say that they are true; two claims that are consistent with each other could both be false, or one could be true and one false.

Claims about unrelated topics can be consistent with each other, as is evident from the following:

3. Paris is the capital of France.
4. It is raining in London today.
5. Whales are mammals.

Claims are inconsistent with each other if it would not be possible for them to be true at the same time, for example:

6. James and Sally are both taller than Joe.
7. Joe is not as short as Sally.

'INCONSISTENCY' and 'CONTRADICTION' are often used as if the terms were synonymous. However, strictly speaking the terms differ in that contradictory claims cannot both be true at the same time and cannot both be false at the same time, whereas inconsistent claims, though they cannot both be true, could both be false. Claims 6 and 7 could both be false, because Sally and Joe could be the same height.

See also: COHERENCE, CONTRADICTION and INCONSISTENCY.

Contradiction

when two beliefs or claims are such that they cannot both be true together and they cannot both be false.

Contradictory beliefs or claims are opposites. They make opposing claims such that they cannot both be true and they cannot both be false from which it follows that one of them must be true and the other must be false.

Here is a simple example:

1. John is in the room.
2. John is not in the room.

Claims 1 and 2 are contradictories, that is, they cannot both be true together and they cannot both be false together. John must either be in the room or John must be outside the room. The two contradictories exhaust the possibilities between them. It is not just that they are opposites; they are opposites and there is no third option.

Contradictories are to be distinguished from contraries which are also opposite claims or beliefs. Contraries cannot both be true together. But unlike contradictories they do not exhaust all the possibilities. So while they cannot both be true together they can both be false together for the simple reason that some third option obtains.

Here is a simple example:

1. John is overweight.
2. John is underweight.

Claims 1 and 2 are contraries, that is, they are opposites which cannot both be true together. It is impossible for one and the same man to be simultaneously overweight and underweight. However, they can be both simultaneously false. They do not exhaust all the possibilities. In this case John's weight may be exactly right for his height and age.

Sometimes a single claim or belief is said to be self-contradictory. In such a case the predicate expression attributes to the subject something which the subject term denies. For example:

1. John's father was a woman.

Here claim 1 is self-contradictory. The term 'father' refers to a male parent and the term 'woman' refers to a female. So the claim contradicts itself in that it asserts that John's male parent was a female. What this means is that the single claim or belief is really equivalent in meaning to a number of other claims which contain contradictory claims. Thus the original claim is equivalent in meaning to:

2. John had a parent.
3. This parent was male.
4. This parent was female.

Here, claims 3 and 4 are straightforwardly contradictory claims. So provided claim 1 is equivalent in meaning to the conjunction of claims 2, 3 and 4 this will show that all contradictions ultimately turn on the existence of contradictory claims or beliefs as defined above.

See also: CONVERSE.

Converse

contains the same terms as another claim but in reverse order.

The converse is like a mirror image of the original; it contains the same terms but reverses their order.

For example:

1. John likes Janet.
2. Janet likes John.

Claim 2 is the converse of claim 1.

In some cases the converse of a claim can be validly inferred from the original. They include both making the inference that no A are B from the premise that no B are A and also making the inference that some B are A from the premise that some A are B.

An example of the first valid inference is:

1. No critical thinkers are poets.
2. No poets are critical thinkers.

Here 2 is the converse of 1 and 2 logically follows from 1.

An example of the second valid inference is:

1. Some critical thinkers are poets.
2. Some poets are critical thinkers.

However, in other cases the converse cannot be validly inferred from the original. Thus it is invalid to infer all B are A from all A are B. Similarly it is invalid to infer some B are not A from some A are not B.

An example of the first invalid inference is:

1. All critical thinkers are poets.
2. All poets are critical thinkers.

Here 2 is the converse of 1 but clearly 2 does not follow from 1.

An example of the second invalid inference is:

1. Some critical thinkers are not poets.
2. Some poets are not critical thinkers.

Here once more 2 is the converse of 1 but 2 clearly does not follow from 1.

Although the term, converse, is primarily applied to claims or propositions, it can also be applied to arguments. When applied to arguments it means two arguments contain the same claims but the order of reason and conclusion is reversed. Thus the converse of an argument which infers the existence of God from the existence of purpose in the world is one which infers the existence of purpose in the world from the existence of God.

See also: CONTRADICTION.

Correlation

a correlation indicates a linear relationship (without implying a causal one) between two numerical variables.

Correlation is a statistical term which refers to a relationship between two numeric variables. The correlation may be either positive (as one variable increases, so does the other) or negative (as one variable increases, the other decreases). There are a number of different types of correlation coefficients which generally give a value between +1 and -1 and which indicate both the nature of the relationship as well as the strength of the relationship.

Two examples of correlations:

1. Height and weight in children – *in general*, across the population, the taller a child is, the heavier they are. This is a *positive* correlation.
2. Annual bonus (£) and absence rate from work – it might be found that the greater the number of days employees take off from work as sick, the lower the amount they receive for annual bonus. This is a *negative* correlation.

Where a correlation exists, it is important to note that the *explanation* for the correlation is indeterminate. Thus, even where 'common-sense' might wish to supply a CAUSAL EXPLANATION, the discovery of a correlation is not sufficient for this to be inferred, or, indeed, the exact nature of any causal explanation. There are usually many possible explanations for the exact nature of the dependency between the two variables, one of which might be a causal relationship. But without further EMPIRICAL and systematic investigation, the explanation remains purely speculative.

For example, it has been found that there is a positive correlation between the amount of time children practise the piano per week and the piano grade exam achieved. Possible explanations might include:

1. Practising the piano causes an increase in achievement on the piano.
2. Children who take higher piano grades need to spend more time practising (because of the greater requirements of the exams in terms of length and difficulty of musical pieces and scales).
3. Children who are naturally more musical are more likely to get more enjoyment out of playing the piano and therefore are more likely to practise, as well as do well in piano exams.

4. Children who organize their time well are likely to be able to find more time to practise and therefore do better in piano exams.
5. Children who are motivated to achieve in general are more likely to try harder and therefore practise more, as well as are more likely to do well in piano exams.
6. It is just a coincidence that there is a positive correlation between the amount of time children practise the piano per week and the highest piano grade exam they achieve.

We can represent these possible explanations diagrammatically, where X = time spent practising and Y = piano grade achieved, and other letters (A, B, C) indicate other variables.

1.   X ⟶ Y

2.   Y ⟶ X

3.   A ⟶ X ⟶ Y

4.   B ⟶ X ⟶ Y

5.

            C
        X   Y

6.   X   Y

While 1 represents the common-sense explanation, it can be seen that all of the above are PLAUSIBLE explanations for the correlation between the two variables (though not an exhaustive list). Without further investigation and analysis, it would be impossible to determine which explanation has the most TRUTH value.

There are broader and more everyday uses of the term correlation, which often describe some type of association between two things. These more everyday usages include:

- the co-occurrence of events; for example, riots are more likely to occur during unusually hot summers
- changes in the incidence rates which co-occur over time; for example, the increase in the use of mobile phones and the increase in diagnosis of brain tumours.

Although more everyday uses of the term correlation might not satisfy the more statistical definition, the same care needs to be taken to avoid inferring a causal explanation.

Corroboration

additional evidence from an independent source that gives direct support to another's claim.

Independent EVIDENCE that agrees with another CLAIM can be said to be corroborating EVIDENCE. For example, if one source claimed that 5.2 per cent of the UK population are on the DNA database and another claimed that 4 million people are on this database, the latter would be corroboration providing that 4 million represents 5.2 per cent of the UK population. To corroborate is to say the same thing, and these do.

Corroboration does not prove the truth of a claim; however, it does provide grounds to say that the CREDIBILITY of the original claim has been strengthened by additional evidence. But there are two important conditions which have to both be met. Consider the following example of spurious corroboration:

> In the twentieth century there were many claims about spinach being so rich in iron, that eating a portion of it was equivalent to eating a portion of

red meat. As well as spawning the cartoon character Popeye, such claims proliferated. They were repeated and recycled in many reputable textbooks, publications, and war-time dietary propaganda in the US, all of which, of course, appeared to corroborate each other. Spinach consumption dramatically increased. But all the claims could, ultimately, be traced back to a single original document from the 1870s which had, in fact, contained a misprint – a decimal point in the wrong place, inflating spinach's apparent iron content tenfold. In fact, the iron content of spinach is no different to other green leafy vegetables such as Brussels sprouts or cabbage.

Thus, the apparent corroboration between these text books was entirely spurious.

This illustrates that two conditions should be met for corroboration to have a positive impact upon credibility. First, the additional claimant(s) should be reliable and second, the sources should be independent of one another. In the example described above, some of the publications were indeed reputable and thought of as reliable; however, they were not independent.

See also: INCONSISTENCY.

Counter-argument

an argument which reaches a different or opposite conclusion from the argument under consideration.

The following example appears in the entry for 'ARGUMENT STRUCTURE':

A. In all civilized societies there are laws prohibiting assault. Sport is no exception, or at least it shouldn't be. Therefore no sport should be permitted in which the object is to inflict injury.

Argument A might be *countered* as follows:

B. The laws prohibiting assault cannot be applied to contact sports, especially combat sports such as boxing and wrestling. In these activities the players are willing participants who know the risks and accept the inevitable injuries. In a free society they should have the right to make these decisions.

Argument B takes a different direction and reaches a very different conclusion from argument A. Moreover argument B opposes, or challenges argument A. That makes it a counter-argument.

Often in argumentative text the author presents or refers to one argument or viewpoint and then launches his or her own argument against it. For example:

C. In all civilized societies there are laws prohibiting assault, and rightly so because people have an absolute right not to be hurt or injured by other members of society. However, sport – especially combat sport – is an exception because in these activities the players are willing participants who know of the risks and accept the inevitable injuries. In a free society they should have the right to make these decisions.

In argument C the case being made is similar to B, only the author places it in the context of a response to A. When analysing C it would be wrong to call the first sentence a 'counter argument'. The right way to describe the role of this sentence is as context, target, introduction, background or some such label.

Counter-arguments are typically found in dialogue, where one speaker makes a claim or case and another argues against it. In such contexts it is quite normal to find counter-arguments responded to by *counter*-counter-arguments, followed by counter-counter-counter-arguments. . . and so on.

Sometimes the author of an argument will *anticipate* a counter-argument. For example, the author of C might rephrase the last sentence:

Of course, some people think it is wrong to invite injury and that it is wrong to injure someone even if they do invite it. They are wrong, because the most important rights of all are our rights to choose, and if a fighter chooses to make his living by punching and being punched, it is not the business of the law to deny him the right. . . etc.

Again we need to be careful how we designate the two parts of this text (and texts like it). We could say that each is a counter-argument to the other. Or, being more precise, we could say that the first is a *target* argument and the second a counter to it.

Counter-assertion

a claim which challenges, or asserts the opposite of, some other claim.

For example, if I assert that violence in cinema should be banned whether people enjoy it or not, a counter-assertion would be that if people want to watch violence in cinema such films should be permitted.

A counter-assertion differs from a counter-argument in that in a counter-argument reasons are given, as well as assertions. An assertion need not be accompanied by any reasons.

Counter-example

an example which runs counter to a trend or throws doubt on a generalization or alleged correlation.

Consider the categorical claim that all snakes are venomous. A counter-example is any snake which is not venomous (e.g. a python). The existence of one non-venomous snake would be sufficient to falsify the claim.

Counter-examples are useful in refuting certain arguments and/or in testing HYPOTHESES. Imagine a theory being put forward that house prices are a reliable indicator of the quality of local schools, on the strength of a survey showing that wherever average house prices were above a certain level, the local schools had above average standing in the league tables and *vice versa*. A counter-example would be an area with very high house prices and poor schools or an area with good schools and low house prices.

In the face of such an example various options are available. One would be to abandon the hypothesis altogether. Another would be to weaken (moderate) the original claim, for example, by replacing it with 'House prices give *some* indication of the quality of local schools'. A third would be to retain the hypothesis and seek some way of *explaining away* the counter-example. This could be done by questioning whether that part of the survey had been conducted properly, or whether league tables are a reliable guide to the quality of educational provision in a school in every case.

Although a counter-example is not always a conclusive reason for rejecting a hypothesis outright, genuine anomalies must be taken seriously, and the temptation to produce AD HOC responses just to protect a hypothesis should be resisted. For instance, it would be ad hoc to dismiss examples of good schools in poor areas on the grounds that their success must have some special explanation, such as extra government money, which disqualifies them from inclusion in the survey. This is tantamount to saying that the only examples which count are those which favour the hypothesis! Reasoning of this kind is not uncommon when a cherished theory is under attack from a counter-example and learning to recognize it is an important critical skill.

See also: GENERALIZATION and STRENGTH AND WEAKNESS.

Creative thinking

involves producing innovative or imaginative ideas.

Creative thinking involves thinking about, for example, an object, concept or question in an innovative or original way. This may involve an element of 'confluence', such as detecting the connection between two seemingly unrelated ideas, or combining known elements or concepts in a novel way.

CRITICAL THINKING is not the enemy of creativity. The two sets of skills and dispositions, though mainly distinct, can exist side by side and are complementary. Within the domain of Critical Thinking and wider thinking skills, creative thinking is useful in terms of, for example, providing alternative explanations and solving problems.

Further reading

Sternberg, R. (1999), *A Handbook of Creativity*. Cambridge: Cambridge University Press.

Credibility

the extent to which a claim or source of information (e.g. a document, a person or an organization) is believable.

The term 'credible' is used in Critical Thinking in its normal sense, that is, 'believable' or 'trustworthy'. A judgement that a claim is credible is a judgement that there is good reason to believe it. This is not tantamount to saying that the claim is true.

The following criteria need to be considered when the credibility of a claim or a source is to be assessed:

1. Is the source of the information reliable, that is,
   - is the person from whom the information comes known to be generally truthful and trustworthy (reputation)?
   - would the person lose something by being truthful, or gain something by deceiving others (possible VESTED INTEREST)?
   - is the person in the position to have the relevant knowledge (relevant experience or EXPERTISE)?
   - are there factors (see, OBSERVATIONS, RELIABILITY OF) which could interfere with the accuracy of the person's judgement?
2. Does the claim have PLAUSIBILITY, that is, is it the kind of thing that could be true or could happen?
3. Is there CORROBORATION of the claim from an independent source?

If the source can be judged to be reliable in accordance with the above criteria, and the claim is plausible, then the credibility of the claim is high. If there is also corroborating evidence from another reliable source, then credibility is further strengthened.

See also: CORROBORATION, EVIDENCE, EVALUATION , OBSERVATIONS, RELIABILITY OF, PLAUSIBILITY and VESTED INTEREST.

Critical Thinking

Critical Thinking is the analytical thinking which underlies all rational discourse and enquiry. It is characterized by a meticulous and rigorous approach.

As an academic discipline, it is unique in that it explicitly focuses on the processes involved in being rational.

These processes include:

- analysing arguments
- judging the relevance and significance of information
- evaluating claims, inferences, arguments and explanations
- constructing clear and coherent arguments
- forming well-reasoned judgements and decisions.

Being rational also requires an open-minded yet critical approach to one's own thinking, as well as that of others.

There are many definitions of Critical Thinking. However, the definition above represents one derived by a number of UK Critical Thinking experts.

This definition closely relates Critical Thinking with rationality. Thus, in one sense, Critical Thinking, as an *activity*, is ubiquitous; all rational discourse and enquiry involves the activity and application of Critical Thinking. Both formal (subject domains across the science–humanities divide) and informal (everyday) rational discourse and enquiry rely upon ANALYTICAL and reasoned thought.

The definition highlights that one of the main features of Critical Thinking is that it is analytical. Many of the processes and skills of Critical Thinking rest upon the ability to be analytical, to be able to dissect arguments and information.

Good Critical Thinking is exemplified when the thinking is rigorous and meticulous. That is to say that Critical Thinking is not passive, automatic, spontaneous or reactive in manner, but is active, careful and thorough.

Although Critical Thinking, as a form of thinking, can be acquired and exercised through incidental exposure in one's general educational experience, the reference to Critical Thinking as an academic discipline acknowledges that this is a set of skills which can be explicitly and purposefully learnt and taught. Critical Thinking comprises a number of processes involved in being rational. These processes are often implicit, hidden or tacit. Studying Critical Thinking makes these processes unconcealed and explicit. Therefore, though a person who has had an absence of any overt Critical Thinking teaching might still be equipped with a range of Critical Thinking skills, explicit teaching of Critical Thinking can introduce awareness of, or increase proficiency in the processes involved in being rational. Thus, an important aspect of Critical Thinking is that of METACOGNITION. The value of the discipline is that it can be applied in all contexts in which reasoning occurs or should occur.

Critical Thinking emphasizes processes – hence the inclusion in the definition of five of the most significant of the many processes of rationality – which encompass the skills and sub-skills outlined in the taxonomy.

Open-mindedness is an important aspect of Critical Thinking. Being able to set aside one's own views is a prerequisite for a thorough examination of another's argument, allowing apprehension of other frames of reference. Furthermore, open-mindedness allows a person to acknowledge that their own views may be unsupported or even wrong. Critical Thinking involves a fair-minded assessment of evidence, rather than seeking to support or confirm one's own views.

The definition indicates that Critical Thinking is a set of skills which one applies not only to other people's reasoning, but also to one's own. Being rational requires self-reflection and self-correction. In other words, it requires analysis, evaluation and elucidation of one's own thinking with the aim of greater internal COHERENCE and accuracy in one's own reasoning.

See also: REASONING.

Further reading

Fisher, A. and Scriven, M. (1997), *Critical Thinking: Its Definition and Assessment*. Point Reyes, CA: Edgepress.

Black, B., Chislett, J., Thomson, A., Thwaites, G. and Thwaites, J. (2008), *Critical Thinking – A Definition and Taxonomy for Cambridge Assessment: Supporting Validity Arguments about Critical Thinking Assessments*. Paper presented at the 38th International Association for Educational Assessment, Cambridge.

Deduction / deductive reasoning

a form of reasoning which – if it is SOUND *reasoning – provides us with certainty. Non-deductive reasoning can provide only high probability or at best near certainty.*

The most famous example of deductive reasoning is:

1. *All men are mortal; Socrates is a man; so Socrates is mortal.* It can easily be seen that if the two premises are true, the conclusion cannot possibly be false. That means this argument is not only deductive but also deductively *valid*. Compare the following example, which looks similar but is very different:
2. All men are mortal; Socrates is mortal, so Socrates is a man.

This argument has a deductive form but it is invalid / not valid. Socrates could be the name someone has given to their pet guinea pig, in which case both premises would still be true but the conclusion would not. Any argument form that *could* have true premises and a false conclusion is invalid.

The following argument is neither deductive nor strictly valid:

3. For several million years ice ages have occurred on regular cycle, with each ice age itself lasting for about 100,000 years and separated from the next by a period – called an 'interglacial' – lasting between 10,000 and 15,000 years. The present interglacial began over 10,000 years ago. Therefore we are over half way back towards ice-age conditions. (John Gribbin (1999), *The Little Book of Science*. Source (adapted). London: Penguin, p. 51.)

Although the last example is a *good* argument in the sense that its reasons give very strong support for its conclusion, its conclusion is based on a prediction, which means that it could be false this time round, despite the evidence of regular cycles in the past. Humans may have messed up the climate so much that ice ages are a thing of the past – unlikely, but not inconceivable.

Deductive validity is like a guarantee. However, in providing such a guarantee, deductive reasoning can seem artificial and/or rather trivial and uninformative.

Example 1 is a case in point; if we know Socrates is a man, we know he is mortal. We don't need the whole argument to convince us.

Here is another deductive argument, which you may recognize from some of the other entries:

4. If these banknotes were genuine they would all have different serial numbers. These all have the same serial number. Therefore they are not all genuine.

As well as being deductive this is a valid argument because, if the first two sentences are true, the last one cannot be false. But in real-life conversation ordinary people would rarely, if ever, bother to spell it out in full like this. They would be much more likely to say any one of the following:

a. These banknotes have the same serial number so they are not all genuine. (Implying that all genuine notes have different numbers.)
b. These banknotes are not all genuine. If they were they would have different serial numbers. (Implying that they haven't got different numbers and are that they not genuine.)
c. If these banknotes were genuine they would all have different serial numbers. (Implying that they haven't got different numbers *and* are that they are not genuine.)

The last three examples can each be recognized as deductive in their *underlying* reasoning. But to analyse them fully in a standard form, the unstated assumptions and/or implied conclusion need to be included:

Example 4: standard form

All genuine banknotes have different serial numbers.

These bank notes all have the same numbers.

These banknotes are not all genuine.

See also: INFERENCE.

Definition

stating clearly and concisely the meaning of a word or phrase/a clear and concise statement of the meaning of a word or phrase.

One purpose of constructing arguments is to communicate one's reasoning process to others, often in order to convince them of a point of view. Thus it is important that the intended audience understands what is said or written. Any uncommon words, words with a technical meaning, and words which are being used in a specific and unusual sense should be defined by the speaker or writer.

Some definitions are given in terms of NECESSARY AND SUFFICIENT CONDITIONS; for example, 'mother' may be defined as 'a female who has given birth to offspring'. Being female and having given birth to offspring are both necessary for someone to be a mother in the biological sense, and taken together they are sufficient for someone to be a mother in this sense.

Some words or phrases are difficult to define in terms of necessary and sufficient conditions; the word 'sport' is one such example. There is a cluster of characteristics for sport – for example, being competitive, involving physical activity, being indulged in for pleasure – which may not all apply to all the activities we call sport. Such words can be defined in terms of what the philosopher Wittgenstein called 'family resemblances', that is, a set of characteristics typical of, though not essential for, each particular activity that they include. This type of definition can be appropriate for some illnesses, a fact which may confuse those who are not experts in the field of medicine. For example, schizophrenia would be defined by experts in terms of a set of characteristics or behaviours, not all of which would be present in all sufferers, so that two people suffering from schizophrenia may share no common characteristic. Thus we should be aware that even some technical terms cannot be defined in terms of necessary and sufficient conditions.

Definition is often helpful in ETHICAL REASONING, because the reasoning may depend upon terms such as 'rights', 'autonomy', 'justice', and it is not always clear what the author understands by these terms. Defining complex concepts such as these may require much longer and more detailed accounts than the kind of definition given in a dictionary.

Definition can be assisted by presenting EXAMPLES, as is illustrated by many of the entries in this glossary.

Critical thinkers need to beware of persuasive definition, that is, defining terms in such a way as to imply conclusions that have not been supported by good REASONS. For example, someone may define 'smacking' as 'a form of child abuse', in an attempt to persuade us, without engaging in reasoning, that there can be no justification for smacking children.

See also: CLARIFYING MEANING, ETHICAL REASONING, EQUIVOCATION, NECESSARY AND SUFFICIENT CONDITIONS, MISTAKING NECESSARY AND SUFFICIENT CONDITIONS and PERSUASIVE LANGUAGE.

Denying the antecedent

See: FALLACIES, FORMAL and MISTAKING NECESSARY AND SUFFICIENT CONDITIONS.

Dilemma

a choice between options each of which has unacceptable or unwelcome consequences or implications.

A graphic illustration is provided by the novel and film, *Sophie's Choice*. The main part of the story is based in Auschwitz. Sophie, the mother of two children can save one of them from death but not both of them. She has to choose either her son or her daughter, but either choice will be a source of guilt, remorse and profound misery for her.

The dilemma, which in this case is a moral one, would be a false dilemma if it could be shown that there were other choices available to Sophie, and that neither of these dreadful options is truly inescapable. In a genuine dilemma the undesirable options cannot be escaped. Nor could the dilemma be resolved by imagining that there was a *conceivable* alternative for Sophie – say, escaping in the night with both children. That option was not a real (i.e. physical) possibility. Thus Sophie has compelling moral reasons to save her son, and the same compelling reasons to save her daughter, in circumstances where saving her son means not saving her daughter and vice versa. Hence she is faced with a genuine moral dilemma.

Moral dilemmas most commonly arise because of a conflict between different moral principles when applied to the same circumstances. In the moral dilemma made famous by Jean Paul Sartre in 'Existentialism and Humanism', a young man is both obliged to look after his elderly, widowed mother *and* obliged to go away and fight the Nazis; yet it is impossible for him to do both. In this case the principle that one should care for one's parents clashes with the principle that one should fight for one's country against evil oppressors. He is obliged to do one or the other as he cannot do both and yet whichever he does has unacceptable consequences.

Moral dilemmas in the full and proper sense of the term as explained here cannot be resolved without residue. What that means is that even if a judgement can be reached as to which course of action is to be taken, it will remain the case that the action so chosen will still be opposed by powerful reasons which remain in force. To return to the example of Sophie's choice, in the end Sophie decides to save her son. She can and does back up her decision with strong reasons. But this does not mean that the reasons against that choice have been silenced. On the contrary the strong reasons against remain in force and make themselves felt in her legitimate feelings of guilt and remorse.

Empirical/empiricism

EMPIRICAL: *(of knowledge or evidence) derived from experience (i.e. experiment and/or observation).*

EMPIRICISM: *the philosophical idea that all knowledge is derived from experience rather than theory.*

An example from a historical debate about the relative speed at which bodies fall from a height illustrates the distinction between using EVIDENCE from experiment and using theoretical REASONING:

> The Greek philosopher Aristotle had claimed that bodies of different weights would fall at different speeds, that is, that heavy bodies would fall faster than lighter ones.
>
> Galileo questioned this with theoretical reasoning, as follows. Suppose Aristotle's claim were true, then if two bodies of different weights were tied together with 'weightless' string before being dropped, the combined weight would cause the composite body to fall faster than the heavy one alone. However, since the lighter weight would fall more slowly if Aristotle's claim were true, it would slow down the heavy weight, and the two weights together would fall more slowly than the heavy weight alone. Thus Aristotle's claim led to a contradiction, and therefore could not be true.
>
> A different approach to the question, based on empirical evidence, was tried by Giuseppe Moletti in 1576, when he dropped bodies of the same material but of different weights from a height, and reported that they reached the ground at the same time.

Moletti's approach, in common with much scientific research, involved both experiment and observation. Empirical evidence may also be derived solely from observation. One example is the observation of children's behaviour as evidence of their mental abilities. It has been observed that babies who see an inanimate object moving in a stop-start way show surprise, whereas their seeing a person moving in this way does not appear to surprise them. This is taken to be empirical evidence that babies can make a distinction between people and objects, and that they expect people and objects to move in different ways.

Empirical evidence needs to be assessed by critical thinkers in terms of its CREDIBILITY and RELIABILITY.

Epistemology

a branch of philosophy which considers questions about the nature of knowledge and belief.

Epistemology is a large and complex academic subject which goes much wider and deeper than is required by students of Critical Thinking. However, there are some important connections, especially with regard to the JUSTIFICATION of claims and beliefs. Studied at a general, less academic level, (as in Critical Thinking) epistemology is more often referred to as Theory of Knowledge.

This text is not the place for a detailed discussion on a subject as large as epistemology or Theory of Knowledge, but for a summary definition there are few better than the following extract from the entry in the *Stanford Encyclopaedia of Philosophy*:

> As the study of knowledge, epistemology is concerned with the following questions: What are the necessary and sufficient conditions of knowledge? What are its sources? What is its structure, and what are its limits? As the study of justified belief, epistemology aims to answer questions such as: How we are to understand the concept of justification? What makes justified beliefs justified? Is justification internal or external to one's own mind? Understood more broadly, epistemology is about issues having to do with the creation and dissemination of knowledge in particular areas of inquiry.

See also: JUSTIFICATION.

Further reading

For those interested in exploring this subject it is worth reading the whole of the Stanford article at: http://plato.stanford.edu/entries/epistemology/

A short introductory chapter on Theory of Knowledge, suitable for students, can be found in Horner C. and Westacott E. (2000), *Thinking through Philosophy – An Introduction*, chapter 2. Cambridge: Cambridge University Press.

Equivocation

the use in reasoning of a word or phrase that has more than one meaning as if it had only one meaning.

In a typical example of equivocation, the word or phrase has different meanings in different parts of an ARGUMENT (e.g. in two reasons, or in a reason and a conclusion), but the conclusion is drawn as if the meanings were the same. Equivocation may or may not be a deliberate attempt to sway readers to accept a conclusion that is not well supported. When the use of equivocation in argument is deliberate, it is appropriate to regard it as an informal FALLACY.

It is possible that the use of equivocation in the following argument is deliberate:

> Some people want the introduction of privacy laws to prevent the media publishing stories about the private lives of public figures such as politicians. They would allow for exceptions in cases where publication would serve the public interest, for example because the politicians' private lives have damaged their capacity to carry out their public duties. But this ignores the fact that stories about the private lives of public figures are always public interest stories. How else could one explain the huge sales figures for newspapers that carry them? So clearly there is no need for privacy laws because none of the stories about the private lives of public figures would ever come into the category of not being in the public interest.

This argument relies on equivocation over the meaning of public interest. In the second sentence it is used to refer to something the public *ought to know about*. In the third sentence and the last sentence it refers to something the public *likes to read about*. The claim that the public always likes to read stories about the private lives of public figures cannot support the conclusion that stories about the private lives of public figures would always be things the public ought to know about.

It is sometimes claimed that a famous passage from *Utilitarianism* by the philosopher John Stuart Mill contains an example of equivocation. The passage is as follows:

> The only proof capable of being given that an object is visible is that people do actually see it. The only proof that a sound is audible is that people hear it: and so of all the other sources of experience. In like manner, I apprehend, the sole evidence that it is possible to produce that anything is desirable, is that people do actually desire it.
>
> (J. S. Mill, Utilitarianism, Collins/Fontana, p. 288)

In this example the word which is alleged to be an instance of equivocation (i.e. 'desirable') appears only once. Mill is attempting to prove that happiness is desirable in the sense of 'ought to be desired', but his comparison with 'visible' and 'audible' implies that the meaning of 'desirable' is 'can be desired'. Critics claim that in this passage there is equivocation over the meaning of 'desirable' to get us to accept, without good reasons having been given for it, that happiness ought to be desired. Mill may or may not have been attempting to trick readers in this way.

See also: AMBIGUITY, CLARIFYING MEANING, FALLACY (INFORMAL) and CONFLATION.

Ethical reasoning

reasoning about right and wrong, and about which actions are morally obligatory or morally forbidden.

In everyday usage there may be a distinction between 'ethical' and 'moral', such that 'ethical' refers to principles of conduct that are considered correct by a particular group (e.g. a profession), whereas 'moral' refers more widely to principles of conduct for humanity in general.

However, the words 'ethical' and 'moral' are usually used interchangeably in moral philosophy and CRITICAL THINKING. In these disciplines, both 'ethical' and 'moral' have the wider meaning of that which is good or bad, right or wrong in general.

Distinguishing ethical or moral reasoning from other kinds of reasoning requires consideration as to whether the reasoning contains any moral claims, that is, particular kinds of VALUE JUDGEMENT. It is generally not difficult to recognize which claims are moral claims. Consider the following statements, in order to judge which of them make a moral claim:

1. Samir gave nearly all the right answers in the maths test, but he got the last question wrong.
2. The children did wrong: they knew it was not right to torture the cat.
3. You should go to university if you want to get a well-paid job.
4. You ought to be kind to your brother.
5. Euthanasia should not be legalized.
6. In most countries euthanasia is against the law.

In statement 1 the words 'right' and 'wrong' are used in the sense of 'correct' and 'incorrect', whereas their use in statement 2 involves a moral claim about wrong actions. It is easy to see that statement 2 makes a moral claim, whereas statement 1 does not.

Statements 3 and 4 use the words 'should' and 'ought', and thus make recommendations, as do many moral claims. However, statement 3 is not claiming that there is a moral obligation to go to university; it is claiming that it is a sensible thing to do *on condition that* your aim is to get a well- paid job. This can be described as a pragmatic (or practical) recommendation. By contrast, statement 4 is making a recommendation that is not qualified by any practical conditions (e.g. it is not saying that you ought to be kind to your brother to impress your parents or to get him to share his toys with you). It is best understood as making a moral claim, that is, a recommendation that you should do *x* simply because it is the right thing to do.

The topic in statements 5 and 6 (euthanasia) is often the subject of ethical debate, so it may be tempting to regard any statement about euthanasia as making an ethical claim. However, statement 6 is making a purely factual claim, not a moral one. Statement 5 makes a recommendation, and it gives no conditional qualifications; thus it is reasonable to regard it as a moral claim.

An ethical/moral argument is one in which reasons are given for a conclusion which makes an ethical/moral claim. Here are two examples of ethical arguments:

1. Some companies in the USA are now refusing to employ anyone who smokes, even off duty. This policy is totally wrong, and employers should not be allowed to get away with it. They are within their rights to regulate people's behaviour only if that behaviour directly harms others at work. The decision whether or not to smoke at home is a personal matter.
2. Engaging in war is sometimes defended in terms of the right to self-defence. Yet modern warfare is rarely restricted to harming those who are responsible for attacks on others. How many times do we hear reports from war zones of innocent civilians killed or wounded? It is clear that the only morally defensible position with regard to warfare is absolute pacifism, which rules out responding to attack by counter-attack.

See also: ARGUMENT, PRINCIPLE and VALUE JUDGEMENT.

Evaluation

appraising the worth or quality of something. In Critical Thinking, evaluation is routinely performed on arguments – for example, to judge whether or not they are sound or effective – as well as on claims, explanations and evidence.

The evaluation of an argument should be broken down into the following questions:

1. Are the reasons true, or at least acceptable?
2. Does the conclusion follow from the reasons? (Is it fully / strongly / adequately supported by the reasons?)

If the answer to both questions 1 and 2 is 'Yes', we can say the argument is SOUND (or 'good'). But if we seriously question the truth of the reasons, *or* we can see that the conclusion doesn't follow from the reasons, *even if they are true*, then we have to say that it is *unsound* (or 'bad').

It should be noted that the term 'sound' can be used both in a technical and semi-technical sense. In the technical sense it requires the argument to be valid, meaning that the conclusion must follow inescapably from the reasons. In the less formal sense it requires only that the reasons are true /acceptable and give strong, or at least adequate, support for the conclusion. In Critical Thinking it is normal for 'soundness' to be understood in the latter, semi-technical way, and for the stricter meaning to be reserved for Logic.

There are a number of subordinate questions which we can ask in the course of evaluating an argument. For example:

- Are there any recognizable FLAWS or FALLACIES in the reasoning?
- Are there any implicit ASSUMPTIONS which are required by the reasoning and, if so, are they warranted, or unwarranted? If they are *un*warranted, that is, if their truth is questionable, then the argument cannot be evaluated as sound, any more than if one or more of its explicit premises were false.
- Are there any irrelevant or illegitimate APPEALS in the text, for example, to (mere) emotion, or to popular (but unsubstantiated) opinion?
- Are there any items of EVIDENCE used in support of the reasoning – statistical data, statements from observers or experts, photographs etc. – and, if so, what could be said about their RELIABILITY, CREDIBILITY and RELEVANCE?
- Does the author use RHETORICAL or persuasive language in any way that distorts the argument or disguises poor reasoning or false assertions?
- Is there any VAGUENESS or AMBIGUITY in the text which requires clarification or interpretation?

Claims and assumptions also need to be critically evaluated at times – independently or as constituents of an argument. Primarily this means assessing a claim's truth or falsity. However, it is often not possible to say whether or not a claim is *factually* true or false. It may just be an opinion or allegation or value judgement, in which case it may be inappropriate to assign it a truth value. We must use instead terms such as 'plausible', 'credible', 'intuitively acceptable', 'well-supported', 'reasonable', 'widely accepted'. . ., and make this clear in our evaluation. An evaluation may not be straightforwardly describable as simply 'sound' or 'unsound', but may need to be qualified. For example, we may want to reserve judgement on the acceptability of the reasons by saying:

> If we agree with the author's condemnation of . . ., then we have to go along with her conclusion that . . .

Even if a claim is of a factual nature we may still not be in a position to judge whether it is true or false. We may simply not *know*, and have no immediate way of finding out. On such occasions we need to be able to give an author credit for his or her *reasoning* without committing ourselves to acceptance or rejection of the claims. A fair critical analysis may take the form:

> The claims the author makes, if true, give strong grounds for her recommendation. However, they are based on data that may not be entirely reliable. . .

Or:

> Whether the claims the author makes are true or not, they are not grounds for the conclusion. . . We must therefore reject the argument.

It should be noted too that even a true, or acceptable, conclusion does not make an argument sound. This is because a conclusion may be true but not for the reasons given in the argument. For example, someone may accept that the ban on fox-hunting should be lifted because fox-hunting provides fun for lots of people. There are many who might agree with the conclusion, for instance, because they consider it a humane way to control a serious pest, but would not accept that the fun it provides was a good reason for permitting it.

What these observations show is that the critical evaluation of an argument has *two* distinct elements – assessment of the reasoning *and* assessment of the claims – and that these must be *kept* distinct if the evaluation is to be fair and complete.

See also: ANALYSIS and EXTRACTING AN ARGUMENT.

Evidence

information that is a ground for belief, and/or that can establish the truth or falsity of claims.

The above definition best reflects the way in which the term 'evidence' is used in Critical Thinking texts and examination papers, which ask students and candidates to assess the RELEVANCE, CREDIBILITY, PLAUSIBILITY and RELIABILITY of evidence.

There are more specific definitions, for example, in the context of law. The following definition comes from a law dictionary:

> Every type of proof legally presented at trial (allowed by the judge) which is intended to convince the judge and/or jury of alleged facts material to the case.

The term is also used in a specific – and similar – sense by Criminal Intelligence Analysts, the branch of the police whose job is to analyse all the information available in relation to a crime, and to judge which pieces of information will be likely to form the basis of a case in court. Information will not be called 'evidence' by Criminal Intelligence Analysts until it has already been judged to be both relevant and reliable. Up to that point it is 'intelligence' (used in the same sense as it is by the military), hence the title of the profession.

This difference of definition between legal and Critical Thinking contexts is not surprising, since in a criminal investigation, and in a trial, that which is considered as evidence is always considered in relation to a particular case, whereas critical thinkers may need to consider evidence in various circumstances.

Here are three such circumstances:

1. One discovers new information (or information of which one was previously unaware). With such information, the critical thinker will consider its reliability and its IMPLICATIONS, that is, what follows from it, or whether it suggests that some policy should be adopted.
2. One wishes to evaluate evidence in relation to some CLAIM or ARGUMENT presented by others.
3. One looks for and aims to evaluate evidence in relation to a question that one wants to answer for oneself.

The second kind of case involves considering the evidence presented by someone else, and judging its relevance, credibility and implications. It may also involve going on to carry out the third kind of operation. In the third kind of operation it is a matter of looking for 'evidence for' and 'evidence against', so in this context the idea that all information is evidence is not appropriate, because any information that is irrelevant will not be deemed to be evidence. Nevertheless the definition in terms of 'information' is most appropriate to the Critical Thinking context, given the first and second type of circumstance described above.

Evidence can be expressed in a claim, and can function as a REASON in an argument. It differs from EXAMPLE, in that examples in reasoning usually have a merely illustrative role, and can give only very weak support to general CONCLUSIONS. Some examples, usually those of personal experiences, can be described as ANECDOTAL EVIDENCE, which cannot be the legitimate basis for drawing general conclusions. For instance, 'my grandfather smoked for 50 years and never got lung cancer' is anecdotal evidence which cannot support a general conclusion about the connection between smoking and lung cancer.

Various kinds of information can function as evidence. Here is a selection:

- data, presented as graphs, tables of numbers, measurements, percentages and statements about any of these
- objects (e.g. a bloodstained knife)
- audio and video recordings (e.g. from CCTV)
- records showing times of phone calls
- DNA analysis
- information from surveys, questionnaires
- reports of experiments
- claims by witnesses to an event
- claims about character
- claims about what someone has said.

The last item on this list may include second-hand or HEARSAY evidence, where someone presents another person's description of an event. Hearsay evidence is generally considered less reliable than witness evidence of an event.

See also: EMPIRICISM, EVIDENCE and OBJECTIVITY.

Example

an instance given to illustrate, explain or lend some support to a claim.

Examples can be very useful to illustrate and lend support to a claim. Consider:

> Some of the greatest scientific advances stem from a casual observation. For example, in the late eighteenth century, Edward Jenner observed that people working on farms and exposed to cowpox did not contract the deadly virus smallpox. He went on to successfully vaccinate an 8 year-old boy against smallpox by injecting him with cowpox virus. Two centuries later, not only has smallpox been eradicated, but many other infectious diseases such as diptheria and polio, are controlled through vaccination programmes.

Examples can also provide strong support for some specific claims, where only one instance is required. Consider:

> Not all birds can fly. For example, the penguin cannot fly.

However, examples are sometimes presented as providing support, though they may only be anecdotal or insufficient because they are not REPRESENTATIVE of the group or kind in question:

> Smoking doesn't cause premature death. My aunt smoked all her life and lived to over 90. And Jeanne Louise Calment, who is in the Guinness Book of Records, lived to 122 years-old having only given up smoking when she was 117.

See also: GENERALIZATION, ANECDOTAL EVIDENCE, and EVIDENCE.

Expertise

the capacity for sound judgement by virtue of possessing specialist knowledge and/or skills.

One of the factors by which we judge the credibility of a claim is by asking questions about the expertise of its author. Therefore, we should trust the medical judgement of a doctor more highly than an actor who is playing the part of a doctor in a TV medical drama.

Occasionally faith in experts can be misplaced where expertise in more than one area is required. Such was the case of Sir Roy Meadows as the expert involved in the cot-death court cases. Although he was an expert in cot death, he was not such an expert in statistics and the error in his evidence helped the jury to wrongly convict the mothers of murder.

See also: RELIABILITY.

Explanation

a reason as to why or how something is as it is.

The term 'explanation' is also used to denote a structure that looks, grammatically, very similar to an argument. But, instead of having a conclusion which needs reasons to *support* or establish it, it makes a claim which is assumed to be true and gives a reason or reasons to *explain* it.

For example:

1. An apple falls to the ground when it breaks from the tree because there is an attractive force between all objects that have a mass.

Or:

1a. There is an attractive force between all objects that have a mass. Therefore (i.e. for this reason) an apple falls to the ground when separated from the tree.

The word explanation can refer to either the whole of 1 or 1a, or just the sentence which does the explaining:

E. There is an attractive force between all objects. . . .

The other part of the construction, the apple falling – that is, the thing being explained – is often referred to as a *phenomenon*, or just an observation or a fact. Anyway, it is not in doubt. We know it happens; we just want to know why.

Strictly speaking, the explanation E is a HYPOTHESIS. In the case of 1a it is such a well-tested hypothesis that in practice it has the status of a fact, generating another question requiring explanation, that is, *Why* do all massive objects attract each other? But here is another explanatory hypothesis which is not so well established:

2. The dinosaurs became extinct because a huge asteroid collided with the earth.

Like arguments, explanations can be critically evaluated. An explanation is partly evaluated in terms of its *plausibility*, that is, not just whether it is likely to be true but also whether, *if* true, it *would* explain the fact or phenomenon in question. If it would this does not necessarily make it true, but gives it some support as a claim.

More technically an explanation is judged by two criteria, *power* and *simplicity*. A powerful explanation is one that would successfully explain more things than just the phenomenon in question. A theory of gravity certainly does this. It explains how planets remain in orbit, why things have weight, why there are tides, and why people in Australia don't fall off the planet and into the sky! Other words for this are 'scope' and 'range'. A powerful explanation has a wide, explanatory scope, or ranges over many phenomena.

A simple explanation is one which does not require lots of other assumptions to be made to justify it, or to prop it up. Gravity does not score quite as well here, since it requires that somehow objects, some separated by huge distances, can exert an invisible force on one another. In time the theory of gravity may be replaced by a simpler explanation that explains as much or even more about the universe and the matter and energy in it.

There is an important form of reasoning which supports a hypothesis on the grounds that it offers a plausible explanation or the best explanation for one or more phenomena. It is called ARGUMENT TO THE BEST EXPLANATION or ABDUCTION.

Historical note

For centuries philosophers, scientists and others have recognized a principle known as Occam's Razor (after the mediaeval philosopher William of Occam.) The principle broadly states that if we have to choose between two or more explanatory theories then, if all else is equal, we should choose the simplest – in the sense given above. Why? Because, as already noted, the simpler an account the fewer extra beliefs it requires. A classic example was the model of the solar system before the time of Johannes Kepler. The traditional view was that all heavenly motion was perfectly circular and uniform, despite the observed fact that some of the planets appeared to stray or back track at times. These oddities were accommodated by positing a whole series of complicated manoeuvres called 'epicycles', until Kepler came up with the much simpler solution that the orbits of planets are not circles but ellipses. With elliptical motion, relative to the earth's own movement, the apparent changes of direction could be explained much more simply.

See also: ARGUMENT VERSUS EXPLANATION.

Extracting an argument

separating an underlying argument from its natural-language context.

Consider the following simple example:

> Smoking out of office hours is a personal matter. Companies should not seek to regulate the personal behaviour of their staff. So it is wrong for companies to refuse to employ people who smoke at home. We need to boycott these companies.

Simple arguments such as the above are rare and are most commonly found in textbooks introducing students to the basic skills of argument analysis. In real life, in newspapers and journals, arguments are much more difficult to analyse both because they are embedded within non-argumentative material and because they are not always fully explicit. To extract an argument from the wider context which contains non-argument elements it is necessary to identify and isolate elements which are merely scene setting, descriptive, explanatory or rhetorical but which do not serve to add reasoned support to a conclusion.

The following passage can serve as a simple illustration of some of the possibilities:

There has been a significant increase in what can only be described as 'nanny companies' in recent years. We are all used to the state interfering in our private lives telling us what to eat, what to drink, when we can marry and who we can marry! But now private companies are at it as well. Some companies in the US are now refusing to employ people whose private behaviour at home does not come up to scratch! So watch out if you like to smoke at the weekends! No doubt this creeping 'nannyism' both in the state and in the business world is due to our modern obsession with risk avoidance which in turn is due to the neurosis which is endemic in modern secular life. We need to take action now and boycott these firms. It is wrong for them to refuse to employ people who smoke at home. Isn't smoking at home our own private business?

To extract the argument, the main conclusion needs to be located, along with the grounds or reasons that are provided in the text in support of the conclusion. The argument is mainly contained in the final three sentences of the passage. The preceding sentences largely serve the function of scene setting and description albeit in loaded language. To extract the argument leaves the rather bare excerpt:

We need to take action now and boycott these firms. It is wrong for them to refuse to employ people who smoke at home. Isn't smoking at home our own private business?

But it still remains necessary to engage in an element of argument reconstruction, partly because the argument is expressed in natural language rather than formal language. For example, to analyse the passage as an argument it is useful to rephrase the question as a claim so that it reads, 'Smoking at home is our own private business'. Analysis of the argument can identify the main conclusion as 'We need to take action now and boycott these firms'; the intermediate conclusion as 'It is wrong for them to refuse to employ people who smoke at home' and identify 'Smoking at home is our own private business' as a reason supporting the intermediate conclusion.

See also: ANALYSIS, ARGUMENT, ARGUMENT STRUCTURE and PRINCIPLE OF CHARITY.

Fact and opinion

a distinction which is of great importance in assessing claims and their justifi-cation. Facts are truths about the world. Opinions are beliefs or judgements or points of view.

It should be noted that the terms 'fact' and 'opinion' are not opposites. The opposite of a fact is a falsehood, whereas an opinion may be true, or it may be false, or it may be neither. The key difference between a fact and an opinion is that a fact exists whether or not anyone knows or believes it, whereas an opinion is something which is held or expressed by one or more people.

The following examples may help to clarify the relationship:

A. The Moon orbits the Earth.
B. Mars orbits the Earth.
C. There is life on other planets besides Earth.
D. Extra terrestrial exploration is an unacceptable waste of resources in the face of world poverty.

A states a fact; B is false. These two remain true and false respectively what-ever anyone thinks. If someone expresses the opinion that A is false or B is true they are wrong, and that is all there is to it. We can give this assessment of A and B on the basis of overwhelming scientific evidence and observation, amounting to knowledge.

C is either a fact or a falsehood, but with the current state of science no one is in a position to say which it is. There are arguments for and against C, and there are people who have reasons to believe strongly one way or the other. But until some conclusive evidence is found – asserting C or denying it – it remains merely an expression of opinion. Nonetheless we can say of claims such as C that they are *factual in kind*, meaning that their truth or falsity is unaffected by what anyone thinks or believes. Suppose, for example, that there is life on one or more planets in a neighbouring galaxy. If so then C is a fact. The difference is that whereas I can claim A as *knowledge* I can claim C as no more than a *belief*.

D, by contrast, is neither true nor false in any objective, mind-independent sense. It is therefore not even factual in kind, as C is. D is instead a *matter of opinion* or more specifically a value judgement.

The above points are broadly philosophical or epistemological matters. However, they are relevant to Critical Thinking for several reasons. First, the term 'fact' is often used persuasively in arguments. Saying 'that's a fact' is often another way of saying 'that's true'. Asserting that something is true does not make it true, but applying the word 'fact' gives the impression that what is being said *is* true. Conversely the word 'opinion' is often used pejoratively, implying a lesser status, 'That's not a fact, that's just an opinion'. There is nothing illegitimate about using an opinion as a premise in an argument. What the critical reader or listener must look out for is reasoning which passes off matters of opinion as matters of fact, or an expression of belief as a claim to knowledge.

Second, it is useful to point out that many claims that are presented as facts contain at least some element of interpretation. An important skill in Critical Thinking is learning to spot the hidden judgements lurking behind or within claims that appear purely factual. Statements about statistics, averages, data and trends are almost always interpretations, and to ask whether or not they are true is problematic.

Third, it can take more than facts to establish a value judgement. For example, it may be a cast-iron fact that the cost of a manned expedition to Mars is *x* billions of dollars, but we cannot infer from this figure that the expedition is an 'unacceptable waste' unless we tacitly agree on what level of expenditure *is* acceptable, and/or what counts as 'waste' rather than money well spent. And these, certainly, are matters of opinion (or judgement), not of fact.

This does not mean that we must reject any argument simply because some of its premises or assumptions are opinions rather than established facts. It does mean, however, that we need to be aware of the nature of claims made, and take this into account when assessing their justification.

See also: certainty, epistemology, justification and value judgement.

Fair-mindedness

a quality of mind whereby a person will take another's view as seriously as one's own.

Some critical thinkers, for example, Richard Paul (1992), place fair-mindedness at the heart of Critical Thinking. In other words, to be a 'strong sense' critical thinker (rather than 'weak sense', that is, just using reasoning skills as a set of 'moves' in order to win an argument), a person must be able to adopt another person's point of view and explore their argument networks in order to fully appraise their point of view.

See also: Critical Thinking.

Fallacy, formal

an argument form which is deductively invalid but which can appear to be deductively valid to the unwary.

A fallacy is an identifiable argument form or type which is always invalid but which can appear to be valid to the unwary and unsuspecting because of a superficial resemblance to a valid argument form. When the fallacy or invalid argument form superficially resembles a deductively valid argument, it is categorized as a formal fallacy. When the fallacy or invalid argument form superficially resembles an inductively sound argument it is characterized as an informal fallacy.

Deductively valid arguments share common logical forms and it is in virtue of these common logical forms that the particular arguments which exemplify those forms are deductively valid. The specific and particular content of these deductively valid arguments, what they are actually about, is irrelevant to their validity as arguments. Two simple and common illustrations of valid argument forms are those characterized by logicians as modus ponens and modus tollens. Modus ponens has the form:

R1: If P then Q

R2: P

C: Therefore Q.

Modus tollens has the form:

R1: If P then Q

R2: Not Q

C: Therefore not P.

In each case any particular argument which shares this logical form will be deductively valid regardless of what claims the letters P and Q stand for.

A formal fallacy is an argument form which is deductively invalid yet superficially resembles a deductively valid argument. The argument form is deductively invalid when the conclusion cannot be derived from the premises with certainty, regardless of what the subject matter of the argument actually is about. The problem, therefore, with the argument is not with its actual content but with its structural form. Thus corresponding to the two deductively valid argument forms involving the conditional, if. . .then, logicians recognize two argument forms which are deductively invalid. The first of these entitled, 'Affirming the Consequent' bears a superficial resemblance to modus ponens. Both argument forms share the same first premise, both argument forms take as a second premise an affirmation of one of the two variable expressions and both argument forms seek to reach a positive conclusion about the other variable expression. Thus affirming the consequent takes the following form:

R1: If P then Q

R2: Q

C: Therefore P.

Clearly this is a deductively invalid argument form: regardless of what P and Q stand for it is impossible to derive this conclusion from these premises with any certainty. Therefore, to reason in this way is always to reason erroneously. The argument form is structurally flawed. However, because of its superficial resemblance to the valid argument form, modus ponens, it can deceive the unsuspecting and unwary. Hence, it is a formal fallacy.

Much the same can be said of the second formal fallacy involving the logical constant, if. . .then. This formal fallacy is known as 'Denying the Antecedent'. Structurally it bears a superficial resemblance to modus tollens. Both argument forms share the same first premise, both argument forms take as their second premise the denial of one of the variable expressions and both arguments seek to establish a negative conclusion regarding the other variable expression. Thus denying the antecedent takes the following form:

R1: If P then Q

R2: Not P

C: Therefore not Q.

Once more this is a clearly invalid argument. Irrespective of what claims are substituted for the variable expressions, P and Q, it is impossible to derive this conclusion from these premises with deductive certainty. Anyone who argues in this way must be mistaken and confused. In other words, the argument is structurally flawed. Nevertheless the mistake is one which can easily be made by the inattentive because the argument form does superficially resemble that of a deductively valid argument, modus tollens.

What is true of these two types of formal fallacies is true of them all. In each case a formal fallacy designates an argument form which is deductively invalid but which superficially resembles a deductively valid argument form.

See also: FLAW, DEDUCTIVE REASONING, INFORMAL FALLACY, LOGIC and VALIDITY.

Further reading

Bowell, T. and Kemp, G. (2005), *Critical Thinking: A Concise Guide*. London: Routledge.

Finocchiaro, M. (2005), *Arguments about Arguments: Systematic, Critical and Historical Essays in Logical Theory*. Cambridge: Cambridge University Press.

Fallacy, informal

an argument which is flawed not by its form but by its content.

Fallacies are flawed arguments. They may simply result from reasoning errors on the part of the author or from deliberate attempts to persuade the audience to accept a conclusion without good reason.

Fallacies can be divided into the formal and the informal. FORMAL FALLACIES display patterns of reasoning which are deductively invalid but bear a superficial resemblance to deductively valid patterns. A formal fallacy can be recognized by looking at the pattern of reasoning alone. It can therefore be represented symbolically, with the actual content replaced by variables. For example:

All As are B; X is B so X is an A.

This is a fallacy whatever the content, no matter what terms are substituted for the variables X, A and B. For example:

All cats are furry. This cushion is furry, so this cushion is a cat!

In contrast, an informal fallacy can be detected only when the content is known. For example:

The health of people in the UK would be greatly improved simply by eating more garlic. Garlic is a key ingredient in Mediterranean food, and people living in the Mediterranean region are known to suffer fewer heart attacks than northern Europeans.

If this is intended to be an argument, it is a fallacy because it assumes that because garlic is eaten in Mediterranean countries, and heart attacks are less common there, that one is the cause of the other. Even if this is true, the author also jumps to the conclusion that the same effect would be evident in the United Kingdom. Thus, there are at least two flaws in the argument, but nothing in the form or pattern of reasoning which reveals either of them.

Nonetheless, there are kinds of fallacy which are found repeatedly in different arguments so that they can be identified and in some cases named. For example, the first fallacy identified in the example above is the confusion of cause with correlation. This is a very common type of reasoning error.

See also: FLAW, FALLACY FORMAL, GENERALIZATION, SLIPPERY SLOPE, TU QUOQUE, AD HOMINEM, STRAW MAN and REVERSE CAUSATION.

Further reading

Bowell, T. and Kemp, G. (2005), *Critical Thinking: A Concise Guide*. London: Routledge.

Finocchiaro, M. (2005), *Arguments about Arguments: Systematic, Critical and Historical Essays in Logical Theory*. Cambridge: Cambridge University Press.

False dichotomy

restricting the available options to two when there may be more.

A false dichotomy could occur because the author is ignorant of the possible choices, or as a conscious ploy attempts to steer the audience towards a particular conclusion.

For example, to persuade the public to adopt curfews, it could be argued that the government has to choose between either a night-time curfew in areas of knife crime or face the alternative of escalating violence involving knives. Presented in this manner, if these were the only alternatives, the choice would be clear. However, there are many other alternative courses of action such as the option of greater police presence to detect and deter knife carrying. The ARGUMENT presented, although at first sight appears to be giving a clear message, is flawed because of a false division into two alternatives. The flaw is also known as a FALSE DILEMMA as the reader is forced down the route of a difficult choice between two options, both of which have negative consequences, when in fact there are other available options.

While a false dichotomy falsely restricts the options to two, a *restricting-the-options* flaw can restrict the options to any number that is less than the number available.

False dilemma

See: DILEMMA.

Flaw

a deficiency in reasoning.

Within Critical Thinking the term flaw can be used very broadly and widely to designate any deficiency in reasoning.

It can thus be used to cover any of the following weaknesses or failures in an argument:

- formal fallacies
- informal fallacies
- unwarranted or illegitimate appeals
- the uncritical use of statistical data from, for example, polls
- the uncritical use of sources and testimony by giving greater credence to claims than they merit when judged by credibility criteria
- the uncritical use of evidence and examples which fail to be relevant or adequate to the claims they purport to support
- weakness in reasoning when conclusions are too strong for their supporting reasons; and reasons are neither relevant nor adequate to their conclusions
- reasoning from false premises
- reasoning from false assumptions.

Employed as a broad and generic term of disapprobation, the term flaw can also be used within Critical Thinking as a synonym for weakness in reasoning.

See also: CREDIBILITY, EVALUATION, EVIDENCE, STATISTICAL REASONING, RESEARCH METHODS and STRENGTH AND WEAKNESS IN ARGUMENT.

Generalization

a statement asserting something about all members of a group or set.

Generalizations, or general statements, stand in contrast to particular state-ments. For example, it is a generalization to say that the British are reserved, and that Italians are excitable. Neither statement is true of all British people nor of all Italians, and may not even be true of most. Knowing some Italians who are excitable does not justify this kind of stereotyping.

Technically speaking, *any* move from a finite number of examples to a general statement is invalid or insufficiently supported. The fewer the instances, the weaker the grounds for the general conclusion. For example:

> Children at St Thomas's primary school in Kent recently voted the environ-ment as the most important thing to be concerned about in the modern world. This shows how young people are genuinely concerned about the future of the planet.

This is not to say that no generalizations are justifiable. 'The angles of a (Euclidean) triangle add up to two right angles' is a generalization that can-not be faulted, as there are no triangles which are exceptions. Indeed the generalization is true by definition. It is marginally less certain that all objects with mass are subject to the force of gravity, but there is overwhelming evi-dence to support it, even though it is possible that some object, somewhere, is an exception. On the other hand, the claim 'Knife-crime is on the increase in every major city,' though not necessarily false, is not a safe generalization either, since it would only take one city where knife crime was declining to discredit it.

Arguments can often be made more secure by phrasing the conclusion more cautiously. For example:

> A survey of casualties at 25 inner-city hospitals indicates an increase in the number of injuries described as stab wounds, compared with a similar sur-vey 10 years earlier. It is likely, therefore, that knife crime is on the increase in many urban areas.

See also: ANECDOTAL EVIDENCE, REPRESENTATIVE, RESEARCH METHODS and UNWARRANTED ASSUMPTIONS.

Grounds

a reason or reasons for a claim or belief.

The term 'grounds' is a useful synonym for the reasons or premises on which an argument is based. It is normally used in the plural (like 'scissors' or 'trousers'). We do not say of some claim that it is 'a good ground' for a conclusion, even if there is only one. For example, we would say:

The unacceptable behaviour of MPs over expenses provides good grounds for the setting up of an independent watchdog to monitor Westminster finances.

Hearsay

second-hand information from someone lacking direct experience of a particular event.

Hearsay evidence is based on information received from another person, rather than being perceived directly. For example, someone accused of assault might give hearsay evidence that the alleged victim was well known for provoking violence and support this with instances of this provocation that they had heard from others. Without named sources and the ability to investigate these instances, this evidence could only be viewed as 'hearsay' and thus at best only provide weak evidence.

More negatively hearsay can be associated with rumour and gossip, because the claims have been passed around by word of mouth and therefore may be subject to several layers of interpretation, as well as possibly elaboration, omission and exaggeration in the process. Additionally, as the CREDIBILITY of those passing on the information can be difficult to determine, even if they can be identified, these claims are considered as only weak evidence in an ARGUMENT.

See also: OBSERVATIONS, RELIABILITY OF, EVIDENCE, RELIABILITY and EVALUATION

Hypothesis

a possible or probable truth that has not yet been established; a belief that is entertained or held provisionally, awaiting confirmation or proof; a theory.

A hypothesis differs from a claim or assertion in that it is not presented as being true, but as worthy of further investigation. Hypotheses are very often about the causal relations or general laws that help explain phenomena. Take, for example, the hypothesis that personality is inherited. If it is correct, it would explain why children often display some of the same behavioural traits as their parents. A fiercely competitive athlete might have a fiercely competitive businesswoman for a daughter. The father's and daughter's shared personality trait could be regarded as a confirming instance of the hypothesis that personality is inherited. However, it could also be regarded as a confirming instance of the competing hypothesis that all behaviour is learned.

A hypothesis needs to be distinguished from *hypothetical* which is similar to a CONDITIONAL (or conditional statement). A conditional has the form, If P then Q, and may be true whether P is true or not. For example, 'If (P) interest rates fall next year, then (Q) inflation will grow'. This does not mean that *either* interest rates will fall *or* that inflation will grow. It is the *whole* claim – 'If P then Q' – that is true or false. The term 'hypothetical' is often reserved for occasions when P is *not* true. For example, 'If interests rates had fallen last year (though they didn't) then inflation would have grown'. Hypotheses are often expressed as conditional statements or as hypotheticals, but not always.

Hypotheses need to be tested against the EVIDENCE. This involves predicting what would be expected to occur, or be the case, if the hypothesis were true and then investigating to discover whether it is the case. Such activity, performed rigorously, is a major part of SCIENTIFIC REASONING.

Where there is no conclusive proof, a claim remains a hypothesis (or theory) even if the evidence in its favour is overwhelming. Strictly speaking, the theory of evolution is a hypothesis, not a body of fact. So are special and general relativity.

See also: PREDICTION and SCIENTIFIC REASONING.

Hypothetical induction

See: ABDUCTION.

Hypothetical reasoning

reasoning involving conditional or hypothetical situations or statements; considering what would or would not follow from something if it were true.

Hypothetical reasoning, often expressed in the form of 'If . . ., then. . .' (or equivalent – see, CONDITIONAL STATEMENTS), considers what the consequences or implications of something would be *if* it happened to be true – either of something that has not yet happened, or that has not yet been established, or fully accepted, as being true.

For example, it would be reasoning hypothetically to think, or argue:

> If you wait till Monday to buy that suit you saw in the sale then there is a chance that someone else will have already bought it. (Therefore, perhaps you ought to go and get it now.)

Or:

> If she was as patient as you keep saying she is then she would not have lost her temper so easily. (Therefore, she can't be as patient as you say.)

Hypothetical reasoning is used in decision making (as in the first example) and in PROOFS, or REFUTATIONS (as in the second example; see, also, REDUCTIO AD ABSURDUM). In every case it entails suspending judgement on the truth of a claim and focusing on what follows from it logically. There are strict logical rules for hypothetical reasoning patterns. Certain hypothetical reasoning patterns are valid; others invalid (see, FALLACY, FORMAL). Errors are often made with hypothetical reasoning, as humans have a strong tendency to think along invalid argument lines when reasoning hypothetically, and to confuse NECESSARY AND SUFFICIENT CONDITIONS.

Since to reason hypothetically is to ask what would be the case *if* something were true, evaluating the reasoning in an argument necessarily involves hypothetical reasoning. Asking whether or not the reasons give good or adequate support for a conclusion, in particular asking whether or not the conclusion *follows* from the reasoning, is to ask, *if* the reasons were true, does that mean the conclusion will also be, or is likely also to be true? (In a way, *all* reasoning has an (implicit) hypothetical form, as all reasoning involves deciding what does or does not follow.)

Its meaning is not restricted to reasoning from an initial *hypothesis* alone; in other words, it is not the same as SCIENTIFIC REASONING (or the hypothetico-deductive method, the name given to the process of testing a hypothesis by deducing what consequences you would expect to see if the hypothesis were true/ false) although much reasoning in science *is* hypothetical in form. Its meaning is broader, encompassing any reasoning along 'If. . . then' lines.

As mentioned in the entry on CONDITIONAL STATEMENTS, hypothetical reasoning is not necessarily expressed in the form 'If. . . then. . .'. Moreover, whereas all statements that are expressed in the form 'If. . . then. . .' are conditional statements, they are not all hypothetical. *If that had been a triangle, then it would have had three sides* is a hypothetical claim, since it imagines an unreal situation – it says what would have been the case if things had been different to how they really were. However, *If a shape is a triangle then it has three sides* is not a hypothetical claim, as it really is the case that triangles have three sides – there is nothing hypothetical about it. Similarly the following is not a hypothetical statement, since it is not imagining a possible (but as yet unreal) situation, or putting forward an unproved claim:

> If an object is released near the surface of the earth it tends to accelerate downwards in a straight line towards the earth's centre.

Hypothetical reasoning is often compared with SUPPOSITIONAL REASONING, whereby an assumption is put forward, its consequences assessed and a conclusion drawn accordingly. The difference is that the term 'suppositional reasoning' describes a certain method or approach, whereas 'hypothetical reasoning' refers to a particular argument form.

See also: SCIENTIFIC REASONING and SLIPPERY SLOPE.

Imply

*(1) to mean something without stating it explicitly; to suggest; (2) (in logic) to
make true; to entail. The adjective 'implicit' means 'meant (intended) but not
stated'. The noun 'implication' means that which is implied.*

The first of these is the broad, everyday meaning of 'imply'. However, it also
has the second stricter, more formal meaning, especially in logic. To say that
one claim logically implies another means that the second claim follows from
the first; or that if the first is true, then so is the second. These meanings – the
broad sense and the technical one – though related have different applica-
tions, and should not be confused.

Example (broad sense):

> A. 'How did you enjoy the play?'
> 'Well, the stage-set was impressive'.

The second speaker in this exchange states the set was impressive but *implies*
(suggests) that the play was not up to much in other respects. It could be
taken to mean that the acting was poor or the script weak or both. But
since it is not stated that the play was poor, we say instead that it is implied
/ implicit.

Another important example of implication, in the same broad sense, is found
when an argument relies on an unstated, that is, *implicit*, assumption:

> B. Genuine banknotes would all have different serial numbers, so I'm
> afraid these must be forgeries.

This argument is incomplete and invalid without the unspoken assumption that
the banknotes being talked about have the same numbers. But rather than
saying that the argument is invalid we say that the missing claim is *implied*.

In logic, and in Critical Thinking, 'implication' is also used to mean what is
going on in claims with the form, 'If X then Y'. For example:

C. If your sister was in Paris then she didn't commit the crime.

In this statement there are two sentences, linked by the connective 'if. . . then. . .', that is, 'Your sister was in Paris.' 'Your sister did not commit the crime'. But C is not claiming that either of these is true, only that *if* the first is true the second must be true too. In other words the first part *implies* the second.

Note that C is not an argument. It is a conditional statement, or hypothetical. However, claims like C can and often are used *in* arguments. For example:

D. If your sister was in Paris then she could not have committed the crime. As she has cast-iron proof that she was in Paris, she is in the clear.

Usage note:

A common mistake is to confuse 'imply' with 'infer'. It is incorrect to say that my sister's being in Paris *infers* that she is innocent. It is correct to say that her innocence can be *inferred from* her being in Paris, or is *implied by* her being in Paris.

We may also use an even stronger word, 'entail' to mean *logically* imply. 'To be a genuine banknote entails having a unique serial number.'

See also: ASSUMPTION and CONDITIONAL STATEMENT.

Inconsistency

a property of two or more claims such that both or all could not be true at the same time.

See: CONSISTENCY.

Independent reasoning

See: STRUCTURE OF ARGUMENT.

Induction

Induction is a form of non-deductive reasoning leading to conclusions that are probable rather than certain.

The following is an example of inductive reasoning:

> For several million years ice-ages have occurred on a regular cycle, with each ice-age itself lasting for about 100,000 years and separated from the next by a period – called an 'interglacial' – lasting between 10,000 and 15,000 years. The present interglacial began over 10,000 years ago. Therefore we are over half way back towards ice age conditions.

It is also an example of good inductive reasoning. If we take 'several million' to mean at least four or five million, the cycle has now repeated 40–45 times. That is a strong reason to believe that the present interglacial will not exceed 15,000 years and that therefore the next ice age is closer than the last, as the argument concludes. It is not, however, conclusive evidence, because it cannot be assumed that past experience will always be repeated in the future.

Since the premises are true but the conclusion might be false, this argument cannot qualify as deductively valid. Evaluation should therefore be in terms of how probable the conclusion is, based on the reasons; or how confident we can be in the conclusion, given the reasons.

Here, for contrast, is an example of very poor inductive reasoning:

> There are no fish in Lake Luckless. I've fished there twice now and both times I've come away without a single bite.

The premise – the second sentence – gives the reader no grounds for confidence that the conclusion is true, or even probable. Even if someone fished in the lake a hundred times without getting a bite, it does not make it more probable than not that there are no fish in the lake at all, and it would only take one single bite on the hundred and first visit to prove the conclusion false.

See also: DEDUCTION, PROBABILITY and SCIENTIFIC REASONING.

Inference / infer

to draw a conclusion from one or more claims serving as grounds or reasons. An inference is a conclusion drawn in this way.

See also: ARGUMENT and IMPLICATION.

Inference to the best explanation

See: ABDUCTION.

Informal fallacy

See: FALLACY, INFORMAL.

Informal logic

the systematic study of reasoning and argument as it is developed and used within natural languages.

Although the rules of LOGIC are necessary to all valid reasoning and argumentation, they are insufficiently flexible to distinguish between strong and weak arguments in *natural* language. Informal Logic, as a reform movement, grew from this dissatisfaction with formal logic in terms of its ability to equip (undergraduate) students with the tools needed to identify, evaluate or construct real arguments in everyday situations, as opposed to those expressed in formal terms.

The Informal Logic Movement and Critical Thinking are often strongly associated with one another in that both promote logical and rational thought about 'real' arguments in 'everyday' contexts. However, there are generally thought to be some differences. First, Informal Logic is still largely owned and taught by philosophers, whereas Critical Thinking has become more independent from philosophy. Second, there are skills that many identify as Critical Thinking but which fall outside the domain of Informal Logic. These include clarifying meaning, evaluating explanations, checking for bias and selecting material for arguments. Third, whereas Informal Logic focuses mainly or entirely upon skills, many critical thinkers regard the discipline as involving both attitudes/dispositions (e.g. OPEN-MINDEDNESS), as well as skills.

See also: CRITICAL THINKING and PHILOSOPHY.

Intermediate conclusion

the conclusion of a sub-argument which contributes to a complex argument. An intermediate conclusion is thus both a conclusion of one argument and a reason for a further conclusion.

See also: ARGUMENT, CHAIN OF REASONING and ARGUMENT STRUCTURE.

Irrelevance

See: RELEVANCE.

Joint reasoning

See: STRUCTURE OF ARGUMENT.

Judgement

a summative decision which aims to settle a dispute after evaluating and weighing up the conflicting evidence and arguments from all the interested parties.

A story from Greek mythology, the Judgement of Paris, provides a simple illustration of all the key elements involved in coming to a judgement. In the myth, Paris is asked decide between the three goddesses, Hera, Athena and Aphrodite, and come to a judgement as to which of them is fairest. He has to listen to each of them pressing their case. What is true of this case is true of other examples of judgement that involve the following elements:

- A summative decision is reached with respect to a specific and particular dispute.
- It typically requires identifying and applying criteria to be used in evaluating claims.
- It requires determining the relevance and significance of particular claims and/or whole arguments.
- It requires determining the implications of particular claims and/or whole arguments.
- Finally it requires weighing up the overall strength of the conflicting evidence and arguments.

Judgement is essentially practical. It resolves what should be done, who or what should be believed. It is focused on the particular case in hand. It is evaluative. It has to decide what is most significant, most relevant and most important over all. This judgement or valuation of what is most necessary, here and now, in this disputed case involves synthesis, a coming together of all of one's thinking skills, but it also goes beyond them in that the judgement itself is never simply the conclusion of one more particular argument.

See also: SYNTHESIS, DILEMMA and ETHICAL REASONING.

Justification

grounds, for example, for making a claim to knowledge or holding a belief.

Justification is a key concept in Critical Thinking. When we critically evaluate an argument, what we are doing, in more general terms, is assessing
the justification that the reasons give for the conclusion. 'Do the reasons
justify confidence in the conclusion?' is another way of asking 'Is the argument sound?' Of course for an argument to be fully sound, its reasons must
be true, or at least plausible, as well as being supportive, meaning that the
author must be justified in claiming their truth. In turn, we must be justified
in accepting them as true.

So how does anyone justify a claim or belief? Are we justified in asserting
anything that we do not know for certain, and if so what kind of evidence is
needed to provide such justification? These are big and important questions
that have challenged philosophers and others since ancient times. They belong
most centrally to the subject of EPISTEMOLOGY – the Theory of Knowledge – but
they have obvious repercussions for Critical Thinking.

People, of course, give all kinds of justification for their beliefs, some stronger
than others. In many cases it may take more than one kind of evidence to
persuade others that a claim is justified, and the more sceptical the audience
is the more evidence it will take. In many cases there is no amount of evidence
which will give complete assurance, and we must settle for saying that some
claims are justified by no more than the balance of probability, or because
they are more plausible than any competing claim. The highest standard of
justification, short of certain knowledge, is that the truth of a claim is beyond
reasonable doubt. This justifies a jury, for example, in finding a defendant
guilty in a criminal trial. No less justification will suffice.

The following is a roughly grouped list of reasons that are regularly used to
justify (or attempt to justify) claims and beliefs. It is not an exhaustive list, and
many of the categories overlap:

- direct acquaintance: evidence of the senses and memory
- EMPIRICAL evidence: observation and experimental results in science

- the testimony of others
- INFERENCE or deduction from allegedly true premises and reasoned arguments
- explanatory power (see, ABDUCTION)
- COHERENCE or CONSISTENCY with other beliefs
- authority / expert opinion / general acceptance / majority opinion / so-called 'common knowledge'
- PLAUSIBILITY, PROBABILITY and common sense
- lack of contrary evidence
- intuition, conviction . . ..

See also: EPISTEMOLOGY, PROOF (STANDARDS OF) and CERTAINTY.

Further reading

Schick, T., Jr and Vaughn, L. (2005), *How to Think about Weird Things* (esp. chapter 5). New York: McGraw Hill.

Knowledge, Theory of

See: EPISTEMOLOGY and JUSTIFICATION.

Logic

the study of valid forms of reasoning and argument.

Logic begins with the recognition that some particular ARGUMENT 'works' in that the CONCLUSION really does follow from the PREMISES and that another particular argument does not 'work' in that the conclusion does not follow from the premises. Thus it is clear to any reasonable person that the following argument (A) is one which works:

1. All birds have wings.
2. The sparrow is a bird.
3. So the sparrow has wings.

But by contrast it is equally clear to any reasonable person that this following argument (B) does not work:

1. Some birds catch fish.
2. The sparrow is a bird.
3. So the sparrow catches fish.

From this the logician then notes that many other arguments resemble both (A) the particular argument which works and (B) the particular argument which does not work. Thus, for example, the following argument (C) clearly resembles (A):

1. All cats have paws.
2. Felix is a cat.
3. So Felix has paws.

But this next argument (D) clearly resembles (B):

1. Some cats are wild
2. Felix is a cat
3. So Felix is wild.

From these simple points the logician arrives at the two fundamental ideas behind all logic. The first is the idea of logical form. This is the idea that, despite all the differences of subject matter and content, there is a common structure or pattern which is discernible in many different particular arguments. Thus what unites (A) and (C) and a multitude of other similar arguments is their common logical form or underlying structure which can be represented as:

1. All X are Y.
2. This is X.
3. So this is Y.

But (B) and (D) share a different logical structure, one which many other particular arguments also share, and which can be represented as:

1. Some X are Y.
2. This is X.
3. So this is Y.

Having identified the core idea of logical form, the logician can now use this to explain his or her second fundamental idea which is that logical form, the underlying pattern common to many arguments, is what explains VALIDITY and invalidity. (A) and (C) share a logical form and it is the logical form which explains the validity of (A) and (C) in each case. Similarly, (B) and (D) share a logical form and it is the logical form which explains the invalidity of each case. These are examples of particular logical forms. There are others.

CRITICAL THINKING which aims to develop reasoning in students borrows from formal logic an understanding of deductive validity and deductive invalidity which can be explained in terms of common argument forms. However, most arguments in natural language are neither deductively valid nor deductively invalid. Their strengths and weaknesses depend not on purely formal structural features but on their actual content. So in devising strategies for the appraisal and construction of cogent arguments which are neither deductively valid nor deductively invalid Critical Thinking concerns itself with informal reasoning.

See also: INFORMAL LOGIC, PREMISE, VALIDITY, SYLLOGISM, ARGUMENT, ARGUMENT INDICATOR and PHILOSOPHY.

Further reading

Haack, S. (1978), *Philosophy of Logics*. Cambridge: Cambridge University Press.
Read, S. (1995), *Thinking about Logic: An Introduction to the Philosophy of Logic*. Oxford: Oxford University Press.

Mean

a measure of central tendency (or average), the sum of all of the numbers in a set of data, divided by the number of items in the set of data. It is often referred to loosely as 'the average', but since there are other kinds of average, 'mean' or 'mean average' or 'arithmetic mean' is more precise.

It has for a long time been claimed that the mean average number of children per family in the western world is 2.4. Obviously no single family has two children and four tenths of a child in it. The figure is the result of dividing the total number of children in a sample of families by the number of families in the sample.

Mean averages are useful pieces of data on which to base some arguments, but they need to be treated with caution. If there are large numbers of families with five or six children and/or a large number with none, then the mean average does not tell us very much about the probability of a particular family having two or three, which is what the mean of 2.4 seems to tell us.

See also: MEDIAN, MODE, MEASURES OF CENTRAL TENDENCY and STATISTICAL REASONING.

Measures of central tendency

summary statistics identifying the middle or central values of a set of data; sometimes referred to as 'averages'. The three measures of central tendency are MEAN, MEDIAN *and* MODE.

It might seem baffling at first for Critical Thinking to be concerned with mathematics and statistics. But the reason for this (and related entries) is that an important tool for any person wishing to think critically is to be able to evaluate EVIDENCE presented in an argument, as well as use evidence to construct sound reasoning of their own.

Frequently, evidence is presented in the form of averages. To evaluate the typicality, meaning or significance of the 'average' figure, it helps to know what sort of average is being presented (MEAN, MEDIAN or MODE), as well as how and why each of them differ. On occasions, it is possible that an author will mistakenly, or deliberately, select a particular one of these measures of central tendency over another to make or support a particular claim (where another statistic may have provided less or even no support).

The classic example to illustrate the differences between mean, median and mode is that of pay and salary. Consider the following:

The mean average annual salary in the UK is £24,000.

(Data based on a dataset called HBAI (Households Below Average Income) 2006–7, and despite its name, contains data on all levels of income. This is the Office for National Statistic's recommended source for household income.)

Does the mean indicate a 'typical' or 'likely' salary? The mean takes into greater consideration outlying or extreme values (i.e. values very different to that where the bulk of the data lies) than either the median or mode; thus, in this example, the mean value may not be entirely 'typical'. In this case, the majority of people actually earn *less* than this figure, since this average is 'inflated' by the relatively small proportion of the population who command salaries in excess of £100,000. Because they are so extreme, they do 'raise' the mean. The median is less affected by extreme values, since it is the middle value when all the values have been ranked in order (on the same data). When a distribution of values is very skewed (as is the case with salary), the median may be some distance away from the mean but may give a figure more representative of the majority of the data. (In terms of annual salary, from the same set of data, the median annual salary from the same set of data quoted above was £19,500.) Finally, the mode, as the most frequently occurring (i.e. most popular) value, in a large data set is most likely to represent the value where the bulk of the data lies, and is arguably more typical. (In the example given, the modal income is £14,500, quite a difference in real terms from the mean.) However, we should not conclude that the mode is always best – in small datasets, almost any value could end up being the mode almost by chance, and thus little significance should be attached to the modal value in such cases.

Consider the following:

'The people of Britain are better off than they were four years ago, several thousand pounds in fact!' claimed a government spokesman today. 'The mean average income has increased from £24,000 in 2006 to £28,000 in 2010.'

(This example is not based on real data.)

The question is whether the evidence (the increase in mean income) supports the claim that people of Britain are better off. To evaluate this, it is useful for a critical thinker to know how the mean works. In this context, the mean could increase for two reasons: (i) across all levels of income, people are earning several thousand pounds more than they were three years earlier; or (ii) whereas people on lower levels of income may have experienced some small salary increase, the mean reflects that those people on higher levels of income are earning many thousands of pounds more than they were three years earlier, that is, the extremes have become more extreme. In the first case, the spokesman's claim would be justified; in the second, it would be entirely misleading. A critical thinker would have to weigh up which of the explanations for the increase in mean, (i) or (ii), is more plausible.

See also: STATISTICAL REASONING, EVALUATION and JUSTIFICATION.

Median

the mid-point in a series of values, when they are placed in ranking order. It is a kind of average (measure of central tendency). Often it is close to the mean average, but not always.

For example, suppose there are 15 players in a football squad, and the number of goals each player has scored in the season is listed in order.

Assuming the total number of goals is 75, the mean average is then 75 / 15 = 5. The median, however, is only 3, which is not so surprising when you think that at least half the players will have played in defensive positions and therefore will not have had many opportunities to score goals. Also some will have played fewer games than others.

The median is therefore a useful statistic for answering the question, how many goals has a typical player in the squad actually scored in a season? (The mean average would give a misleadingly high answer.)

Note

If there is an even number of variables in a series, the median falls half way between the middle two. For example, had there been 16 players in the squad and the ninth player had scored three goals, the median would have been 2.5.

See also: MEAN, MODE, MEASURES OF CENTRAL TENDENCY and STATISTICAL REASONING.

Metacognition

thinking about one's own thinking.

This term is derived from the Greek μετά ('around', 'by', 'adjacent', 'after'; often used in English to denote an abstraction from another concept) and the term cognition – 'the process of thinking' – derived from the Latin *cognoscere* ('to know').

Referring to a higher order level of thinking, metacognition was a term first used by the psychologist, John Flavell in 1979. Despite some inconsistency in the various conceptualizations of the construct, in the last three decades metacognition has become an area of much theoretical and research interest within the domains of psychology, education and behavioural sciences, philosophy and artificial intelligence.

In general, it is thought that being able to think about one's own thinking offers some advantage in terms of self-regulation, choice of strategy to adopt, monitoring one's own progress at a task, goal attainment and, more broadly speaking, academic attainment.

In terms of being able to think critically, metacognitive skills are most probably involved in improving one's own thinking, for example, spotting weaknesses, inconsistencies and flaws in one's own reasoning. Differing definitions of Critical Thinking vary in the degree of emphasis placed upon metacognition, especially in terms of whether it is a core skill, in operation at all times or a sub-skill deployed on some occasions but not all, and whether it takes the form of a conscious versus a less conscious, background process. In some respects, such differences of conceptualization of metacognition within the discipline of Critical Thinking are also reflected in the differing definitions of metacognition.

See also: CRITICAL THINKING.

Further reading

Fisher, M. and Scriven, A. (1997), *Critical Thinking: Its Definition and Assessment*. Point Reynes, CA: Edgepress.

Veenman, M., Van Hout-Wolters, B. and Afflerbach, P. (2006), 'Metacognition and learning: conceptual and methodological considerations'. *Metacognition Learning* 1, 3–14.

Mistaking necessary and sufficient conditions

the mistake of assuming either that if x is necessary for y, x is sufficient for y, or that if x is sufficient for y, x is necessary for y.

Arguments which confuse necessary and sufficient conditions are one type of FALLACY.

The following argument is an example of mistakenly assuming that a necessary condition is a sufficient condition:

> To make a perfect meringue you have to use a whisk which is operated by hand. If you use an electric whisk, the egg whites won't increase in volume sufficiently. So if you whisk the egg whites with my hand-operated whisk instead of your electric one, your meringue will be perfect.

The argument claims that using a hand-operated whisk is *necessary* for making a perfect meringue, but there may be other conditions that have to be met to produce a perfect meringue (e.g. the correct quantities of ingredients and the right oven temperature, or even the right technique in using the whisk). Thus the conclusion, which assumes that using the hand-operated whisk is *sufficient* for producing a perfect meringue, does not follow.

In the following argument a sufficient condition is treated as if it were a necessary condition:

> Osteoporosis (i.e. brittleness of the bones) is a condition that causes fractures of the bones in some elderly people. Sanjay is over 70, and has just broken a bone in his leg. So he must be suffering from osteoporosis.

The argument states that osteoporosis causes fractures in some elderly people; thus it is claiming that suffering from osteoporosis is a *sufficient* condition for a high risk of breaking a bone when one is elderly. To conclude that an elderly person who has broken a bone must be suffering from osteoporosis, it must be assumed that it is a *necessary* condition, that is, that an elderly person could not have broken a bone if they had not been suffering from osteoporosis. But Sanjay may have broken a bone for the same reason that a younger person could break a bone, for example, simply because he had a very heavy fall.

Arguments that commit the FORMAL FALLACIES of *affirming the consequent* and *denying the antecedent* can also be instances of treating a sufficient condition as if it were a necessary condition.

The structure of affirming the consequent is:

> P implies Q. Q is true. Therefore P is true.

This is also the structure of the following argument:

> If Fred diets, he loses weight. Fred is losing weight. So Fred is dieting.

The structure of denying the antecedent is:

> P implies Q. P is not true. Therefore Q is not true.

This is also the structure of the following argument:

> If Fred diets, he will lose weight. Fred is not dieting. So Fred will not lose weight.

Both these arguments are treating what is claimed to be a *sufficient* condition – dieting – as if it were a *necessary* condition for losing weight. Fred may lose weight due to some other factor, for example, exercising or illness.

See also: FALLACIES and NECESSARY AND SUFFICIENT CONDITIONS.

Mode

a term used in statistics for the value or item occurring most frequently in a series or distribution.

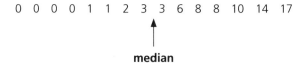

Here is a list of the numbers of goals scored in one season by football players in a squad of 15. The MEDIAN average is indicated above. The MEAN average is 5 (75 / 15).

The *mode*, however, as the most frequently occurring value, is 0. Most players in the squad scored no goals at all.

See also: MEAN, MEDIAN, MEASURES OF CENTRAL TENDENCY and STATISTICAL REASONING.

Modus ponens and modus tollens

Two deductively valid forms of argument.

Modus ponens has the form:

    R1: If P then Q

    R2: P

    C: Therefore Q.

Modus tollens has the form:

> R1: If P then Q
>
> R2: Not Q
>
> C: Therefore not P.

An example of modus ponens might be:

> If it is sunny then I will sit in the garden.
>
> It is sunny.
>
> Therefore I will sit in the garden.

And modus tollens:

> If I am the person guilty of the murder then I am right-handed.
>
> I am not right-handed.
>
> Therefore I am not the murderer.

These are both deductively VALID arguments because, if the premises are both true, it follows that the conclusion must also be true.

See also: DEDUCTIVE REASONING, LOGIC and FALLACY, FORMAL.

Moral reasoning

reasoning about right and wrong, and about which actions are morally oblig-atory or morally forbidden.

See: ETHICAL REASONING.

Necessary and sufficient conditions

NECESSARY CONDITION: *something which has to occur or be true in order that something else can occur or be true.*

SUFFICIENT CONDITION: *something which, if it occurred or were true, would be enough to ensure that something else would occur or be true.*

The following statements make claims about necessary conditions:

- Water is necessary for the growth of plants.
- You have to have a driving licence in order to drive without breaking the law.
- You won't become a good pianist if you don't practise often.
- Working as a solicitor is not possible for someone without a qualification in law.

The above examples show that something can be a necessary condition without also being a sufficient condition. Although water is necessary for plants to grow, it may not be sufficient, since nutrients may also be required. Having a driving licence is necessary for someone to drive without breaking the law, but it is not sufficient because a driver may break the law in other ways such as exceeding the speed limit. Frequent practice in playing the piano may be necessary but not sufficient for becoming a good pianist, because some natural talent may also be necessary. For someone to work as a solicitor, they may have to have a qualification in law, but this may not be sufficient if, for example, they have a criminal record and are excluded on those grounds.

The following statements make claims about sufficient conditions:

- If you eat less you will lose weight.
- The economy will recover if interest rates are lowered.
- Working hard at one's studies will ensure that one passes the exam.
- All you have to do to succeed in the interview is to be self-confident.

This set of examples shows that something can be a sufficient condition without also being a necessary condition. The first example claims that eating less is a sufficient condition for losing weight, but it may not be necessary, because one may be able to lose weight by eating the same amount and exercising more. The next example claims that the lowering of interest rates is sufficient to trigger a recovery in the economy. Economists may dispute this, but even if it were true, it would not imply that this measure was also necessary, since there may be other effective policies. For some people, studying hard may be a sufficient condition for passing an exam, but for exceptionally clever people it may not be necessary. The last statement claims that being self-confident is sufficient for success in an interview, but some people may be successful even if they are nervous, provided those interviewing them can recognize their positive qualities.

Some arguments make the mistake of treating a necessary condition as if it were a sufficient condition, and vice versa. Treating a sufficient condition as if it were a necessary condition can occur in the fallacies of affirming the consequent and denying the antecedent. (See, MISTAKING NECESSARY AND SUFFICIENT CONDITIONS.)

Some DEFINITIONS are expressed in terms of necessary and sufficient conditions. For example, 'brother' could be defined as 'male sibling'. Being male and being a sibling are both necessary for someone to be a brother, and taken together they are sufficient for someone to be a brother.

See also: DEFINITION, FALLACIES and MISTAKING NECESSARY AND SUFFICIENT CONDITIONS.

Neutrality

impartiality, absence of BIAS *or* PREJUDICE.

See also: BIAS and PREJUDICE.

Non-argument

See: EXTRACTING AN ARGUMENT.

Non sequitur

a claim which is presented as a conclusion, but which does not follow from the reason(s) given for it.

The term is of Latin origin, and is translated as 'It does not follow'.

The term is sometimes used in a wider sense than that of the above definition, to refer to a comment that is totally unrelated to a statement that preceded it. For example, if, in response to another's statement that the United States is the world's richest country, someone said, 'The first landing on the moon was in 1969', this latter statement may be described as a non sequitur.

In relation to ARGUMENT, a CONCLUSION may be a non sequitur because the REASONS are irrelevant to the conclusion, as in the following example:

> The weather has been particularly warm recently, and many people are worried about the effects of climate change. So Shakespeare was not the greatest ever British playwright.

In addition to such extreme examples, the conclusion of any fallacious argument is a non sequitur, as is indicated by the definition above. Here is one example of a common INFORMAL FALLACY:

> A study in the USA has discovered a relationship between the number of fast food restaurants in an area and the number of people suffering a stroke. From 2000 to 2003 there were 13 per cent more strokes in areas with 33 fast food restaurants than in those with only 12. It is clear, therefore, that the presence of fast food restaurants is a contributory cause of the number of strokes.

The conclusion in the last sentence is a non sequitur. It does not follow from the EVIDENCE because the proximity of large numbers of fast food restaurants may not be what causes strokes. It is possible that living near fast food restaurants tempts one to eat often in these places, and thereby have a relatively unhealthy diet. However, it is also possible that fast food restaurants tend to be sited in areas housing people on lower incomes, who may be less likely to be able to afford a healthy diet, yet may not eat more often than average in fast food restaurants. The evidence has discovered a CORRELATION, not necessarily a cause. This is an example of the fallacy of assuming a causal relationship from evidence of a correlation.

See also: FALLACY and RELEVANCE.

Objective

independent of subjective opinion.

A simple way to characterize the distinction between objective and subjective is as how things are in themselves (i.e. objective) as opposed to how things are thought to be (i.e. subjective). The distinction is related to that between FACT AND OPINION, as is explained below.

'Objective' refers to facts, and includes:

- Known facts. These can be described as objective, in that they are as they are, regardless of what anyone thinks about them. For example, it is a fact that the Earth revolves around the sun, regardless of what anyone thinks about whether the Earth revolves around the sun. Of course, it could be my opinion that the Earth revolves around the sun, as well as being a fact.
- Unknown facts. We can have opinions about matters that are facts, but have not yet been discovered to be so. For example, it was Ronald Ross's opinion in the nineteenth century that mosquitoes are carriers of malaria parasites, and this is also a fact. He discovered that it was a fact when he dissected a number of mosquitoes of a particular type and, by observing them under a microscope, found that they contained the parasites.

'Subjective' refers to opinions, and includes:

- Opinions that are false, but have not yet been discovered to be so. For example, before oxygen was discovered, there was a widespread, but false, opinion among scientists that certain materials would burn because they contained a substance called 'phlogiston'.
- Opinions such as likes and dislikes. For example, my opinion that whisky has an unpleasant taste.

It is often not possible to say whether what someone expresses as an opinion is objective or merely subjective, because we cannot always distinguish between unknown facts and false opinions about factual matters.

There is widespread belief that all VALUE JUDGEMENTS, including moral judgements, are subjective, or at best inter-subjective, but cannot be objective. This is a matter of dispute in moral philosophy.

See also: ETHICAL REASONING, FACT AND OPINION and VALUE JUDGEMENT.

Observations, reliability of

dependability of eye-witness testimony.

Some claims and arguments rely on observations by witnesses to an event, for example, when an accident or a crime has occurred. Our perceptions of such events can be influenced by a number of factors, such as the ones listed below, which potentially affect the reliability of eye-witness reports:

1. Physical limitations, such as poor eyesight or impaired hearing ability, should make us question the dependability of a witness's evidence.
2. External conditions can make eye-witness reports less reliable, for example:
   • poor visibility
   • extraneous loud noise
   • a restricted line of vision of an event
   • observation of the event from a large distance
   • distractions in terms of other simultaneous events or other demands on one's attention.
3. Previous experience may colour our perceptions. For example, someone who has previously been mugged in a city street during night-time may interpret another's behaviour as threatening if they find themselves in a similar setting.
4. EXPERTISE in observing events, such as policemen and policewomen might have, can also make observational reports more dependable.
5. States of mind and body which can interfere with our perceptual processes, for example:emotions, such as extreme fear
   • effects of substances such as drugs or alcohol
   • beliefs and prejudices, such as general distrust of members of another ethnic group.
   • Critical thinkers need to consider these criteria when assessing evidence based on perception.

See also: CREDIBILITY and RELIABILITY.

Open-mindedness

See: CRITICAL THINKING.

Persuasive language

language that aims to persuade and/ or succeeds in persuading others to accept a point of view.

Although the above definition is neutral with regard to the appropriateness of using persuasive language in REASONING, the term is often used to suggest that someone's reasoning is attempting to persuade by means of forceful words rather than sound ARGUMENT. The purpose of reasoning and argument is often to persuade others to accept a point of view, so in this sense any argument or piece of reasoning can be said to be using persuasive language.

Some reasoning uses persuasive language which critical thinkers need to be able to discount when analysing reasoning or argument. This is generally referred to as RHETORICAL LANGUAGE. It includes the use of emotive words such as 'appalling', 'cruel', and also words aimed at giving respectability to claims, for example 'obviously', 'undeniably' and the like. However, describing language as rhetorical does not necessarily mean that its use in reasoning is a bad thing; it can make dull-sounding arguments more interesting to read, and does not necessarily mask their important message.

Reasoning may also use persuasive DEFINITION in an attempt to elicit approval or disapproval from the reader. For example, if the profit motive is defined as 'legally sanctioned greed', this invites disapproval of those who seek to make a profit.

Persuasive language includes rhetorical devices such as FALSE DICHOTOMY and STRAW MAN.

See also: APPEALS TO EMOTION, FALSE DICHOTOMY, RHETORICAL LANGUAGE and STRAW MAN.

Philosophy

(the study of) the rational and systematic exploration of matters such as existence, knowledge, truth, mind, logic, consciousness, language, morality, justice and aesthetics.

Philosophy is a wide-ranging endeavour with a rich and varied history. Many philosophers' names are well known, for example, Plato, Aristotle,

Wittgenstein and Nietzsche. It is not in the scope of this book to give a full account of philosophy, though it should be helpful to clarify the relationship between philosophy and Critical Thinking.

The closest point of convergence between philosophy and Critical Thinking is the systematic application of rational thought. Critical Thinking is often associated with the 'informal logic movement' – a reform movement in logic with the main aim of promoting logical and rational thought about 'real' everyday arguments rather than the sometimes artificial, formulaic or mathematical approaches of traditional logic.

There are many differences between philosophy and Critical Thinking. Philosophy has a much broader reach in that a wide range of matters might be considered *part of* the study of philosophy; whereas Critical Thinking involves only those skills and processes required for thinking rationally. The object of that rational thinking (that which we think critically *about*) is not part of the discipline and Critical Thinking can and should be deployed in a variety of everyday and academic domains.

Finally, philosophy has been recognized as an endeavour since ancient times, (for more that two and a half millennia), whereas Critical Thinking's beginning as a discipline in its own right, is often ascribed to John Dewey (1909) and his description of 'reflective thinking', though, arguably, Critical Thinking, as a way of thinking and an approach to learning has been around since the time of Socrates and, as such, underlies all rational discourse and enquiry.

See also: CRITICAL THINKING, INFORMAL LOGIC and LOGIC.

Plausibility

(of a claim) the possibility that it is true.

(of an explanation) its capacity to explain the relevant phenomenon.

Everyday usage of the term 'plausible' contrasts with its usage in Critical Thinking, in that in everyday conversation 'plausible' may be applied to people. One may say that someone is 'a plausible speaker', meaning that the speaker appears to be trustworthy. In some cases the term may be used with the connotation that the appearance of trustworthiness is an illusion; for example, we may talk about 'a plausible rogue'.

Because judgements about the plausibility of a person are based on appearance (e.g. facial expression and tone of voice) rather than well-established criteria that can indicate whether someone is telling the truth or being dishonest, the term 'plausibility' is generally reserved in Critical Thinking for claims and explanations. It may also be applied to predictions, in relation to the question as to whether what is predicted is the kind of thing that could happen.

Thus, for critical thinkers, plausibility is distinct from RELIABILITY, in that judgements of reliability can be made about persons as well as claims, and also that characteristics of persons (e.g. reputation and expertise) are relevant to questions about reliability. Both plausibility and reliability need to be considered when assessing the CREDIBILITY of evidence and claims.

Judging plausibility of claims, predictions and explanations requires considering how they fit with existing knowledge. Given that our knowledge is always limited, a judgement that a claim or explanation is plausible (i.e. fits with existing knowledge) cannot give conclusive support. With explanations, judging plausibility also involves assessing whether the explanation could explain the claim or phenomenon. In some cases there may be alternative explanations which are equally plausible.

See also: CREDIBILITY, EXPLANATION, PROBABILITY and RELIABILITY.

Post hoc, ergo propter hoc

the fallacious claim, or assumption, that because x occurred after y occurred, y must have been the cause of x. Usually shortened to 'post hoc'.

The literal meaning of this Latin term is 'after this, therefore because of this'.

The meaning of the term can be illustrated by the debate about a link between the measles, mumps and rubella (MMR) vaccine and autism:

The debate began in 1998 when an article in a medical journal claimed to have evidence that giving children the MMR vaccine caused autism. Subsequently the research upon which this claim was based has been shown to be flawed, and most scientists now agree that there is no causal link. Many parents of autistic children were inclined to believe that there was a link because the first signs of autism in their children occurred soon after they had received the injection.

Although it is a common human response to make the *post hoc* (ergo propter hoc) assumption in relation to all kinds of occurrences, critical thinkers need to be aware that the mere fact of *x* occurring after *y* does not establish that there is a causal connection. The cause of autism is not yet known, but scientists believe that some children may have a predisposition for it. The EXPLANATION for the appearance of symptoms soon after MMR injections may be that these injections are generally given at around the age of one, and that this is the age when autism becomes evident in the child's behaviour. This example illustrates the importance in CRITICAL THINKING of considering alternative explanations.

See also: CAUSAL EXPLANATION, CAUSE AND EFFECT, CORRELATION, EXPLANATION, FALLACIES and AD HOC.

Prediction

a claim about some future outcome, or an outcome that is as yet unknown.

Since predictions are claims about something that is not yet known, they are not facts. Even if they turn out to be correct, they were not facts at the time the predictions were made.

Having said this, some predictions are more PLAUSIBLE than others. As with other uncertain claims, predictions need to be assessed in Critical Thinking according to the grounds for believing them; that is, by considering the strength of evidence that suggests whether or not the prediction is likely to turn out to be correct.

Predictions are important in SCIENTIFIC REASONING. Scientists make predictions when testing HYPOTHESES. For example, Galileo's hypothesis that in a vacuum all objects fall at the same rate, (regardless of size, mass or shape), would be supported by the prediction that if a hammer and a feather were dropped simultaneously on the moon, they would land simultaneously. David Scott, commander of Apollo 15, demonstrated that the prediction was correct and therefore provided a confirming instance of the hypothesis. Although this does not *prove* the general hypothesis – there might be other objects that fall at different rates – it supports or strengthens it. Had the feather and hammer landed at different times, the hypothesis would have been disconfirmed, meaning that either it was false or that some unforeseen circumstance had caused the discrepancy.

Predictions are also used in decision making, when weighing up the likely consequences of different courses of action.

See also: FACT AND OPINION, CLAIM, CONDITIONAL CLAIMS/STATEMENTS, CORROBORATION, REFUTATION and RESEARCH METHODS.

Prejudice

a fixed opinion or viewpoint which is not based on reason or experience, and which is resistant to counter-argument or evidence.

In Critical Thinking, as in normal usage of the terms, 'BIAS' and 'prejudice' may be used interchangeably to refer to a view held without fair and objective consideration of the facts. However, the word 'prejudice' is often used in the stronger sense of an opinion which remains fixed no matter what evidence is brought against it.

Although a bias or a prejudice can be either in favour of or against a particular viewpoint, the word 'prejudice' is often used to refer to preformed negative judgements about another person or social group.

The fact that someone is prejudiced does not entail that their viewpoint is mistaken; merely that it has been adopted uncritically, without objective consideration of the facts.

See also: BIAS.

Premise

a claim from which a conclusion is drawn.

A premise literally means a starting point and refers to a CLAIM from which one makes an INFERENCE to something else.

ARGUMENTS are traditionally described as being made up of premises and a CONCLUSION. Thus in the following argument:

1. All footballers are athletes.
2. All athletes are disciplined.
3. Therefore all footballers are disciplined.

Arguments 1 and 2 refer to the premises and 3 refers to the conclusion.

In Critical Thinking a premise is now usually referred to as a REASON.

See also: REASON.

Further reading

Quine, W. V. (1980), *From a Logical Point of View*. Cambridge, MA: Harvard University Press.

Quine, W. V. (1960), *Word and Object*. Cambridge, MA: MIT Press.

Presupposition

a necessary condition or implicit assumption; something that must be sup-posed in order for something else to be true or believable.

'X *presupposes* Y' means that if someone believes X, they must also believe or accept Y. Consider the following:

> Televised debates between the leaders of the main political parties are planned for the first time in the run-up to the next election. This is bound to have a marked effect on the way people vote.

It would be reasonable to respond to this by saying, 'That presupposes that people will watch the debates. If they don't it won't make any difference'.

In Critical Thinking the term 'presupposition' means practically the same as an (implicit) assumption.

See also: ASSUMPTION.

Principle

a rule that applies to numerous circumstances or cases.

There are different kinds of principle; for example, the laws of science, basic tenets of economics, legal rules and fundamental ethical/moral beliefs. What they have in common is that they have general applicability.

Laws of science are general scientific claims (e.g. Boyle's law) that are accepted as true by scientists on the basis of experiment and observation. Economic principles (e.g. the law of diminishing returns) are general beliefs put forward by economists on the basis of observation of how economies operate. Legal rules are usually decided by governments on the basis of the kind of society they want. In relation to all these, COUNTER-EXAMPLES that become evident in applying the principle to a particular case can lead to modification or abandonment of the principle.

The same is true of ethical principles, which often appear in reasoning about how people should behave, or what policies governments should adopt. Suppose someone puts forward the principle 'One should never cause pain to others', and is reminded that nurses giving injections to babies cause pain, but that they do so for very good reason, and for the eventual benefit of the babies themselves. The principle may then be abandoned or perhaps modified by adding 'except when doing so will benefit the person who suffers the pain'.

Ethical principles are often expressed as recommendations, using the words 'should/should not' or 'ought/ought not'. They can also be expressed in terms of right and wrong; for example, 'It is wrong to kill'. Some ethical principles have wider scope than others, that is to say, they are more general in their applicability. Those with wider scope may be used to justify those with narrower scope. Someone offering the claim that we should not have been involved in the Iraq war may do so on the basis of the principle that killing civilians is wrong, and, if asked to justify that, may appeal to a more general principle that killing innocent people is always wrong.

Moral philosophy seeks to identify the most general ethical principles which could be used as the basis for all decisions that have to be made on ethical issues. Are there principles of such generality that they can justify, for example, the principle that killing is wrong, or the principle that we should avoid causing harm to others? Two famous principles have been offered; one by Immanuel Kant, and one (known as Utilitarianism) by John Stuart Mill. Utilitarianism concentrates on the consequences of actions; modern utilitarians express their principle as 'We should adopt the course of action most likely to maximise the interests of those affected'. Kant's theory concentrates on the actions themselves; his principle can be expressed as 'You should act towards others only in ways which you would accept as morally permissible in others' actions towards you'.

To evaluate principles, we can consider a range of cases to which the principle must apply, and judge whether such cases suggest that the principle needs to be modified or abandoned.

There is one particular principle, not an ethical principle, which can be more appropriately described as a rule for critical thinkers when they are in the process of analysing an argument. It is called the PRINCIPLE OF CHARITY, and can be summed up as follows: if the argument you have identified is a terribly weak argument, then assume that the author, as a rational thinker, was not intending to present this argument.

See also: ANALYSIS, COUNTER-EXAMPLE, ETHICAL REASONING and PRINCIPLE OF CHARITY.

Principle of charity

a guideline for interpreting texts, such that the reader should – for example, in an argument – interpret the text on the assumption that the author is an intelligent person and rational thinker. In the case of reasoning, therefore, we should look for the strongest version of an argument that we can legitimately extract from the text, not the weakest.

What a critical interpreter should not do, according to the principle of charity, is underrate an argument simply to make it easier to refute. This would be prejudicial and would also commit the FALLACY known as the 'STRAW MAN'. In effect, applying the principle of charity is the opposite of a straw man. It requires that where two or more interpretations of a text are possible we should, as a rule, select the best, the one most likely to persuade and certainly one that is valid over one that is not.

The principle of charity also applies when deciding whether or not a text is an argument in the first place. A seemingly contentious text can often turn out to be something less than a fully-fledged argument. It may just be a list of ideas or assertions; it may be speculation. It may even be an explanation rather than an argument. What would be wrong under the principle of charity would be to say, 'This is a very poor argument' when a much fairer interpretation would be to say it was not an argument at all, and was probably not intended as one.

The principle of charity is one of the most effective tools for critical analysis and evaluation because it reminds us to be FAIR-MINDED. 'Charity' in this context does not mean 'kindness'. It means fairness and respect for the authors of the texts we subject to criticism.

See also: EXTRACTING AN ARGUMENT and PRINCIPLE.

Probability

a measure or estimate of how likely a claim is to be true.

Claims about probability are claims about how likely something is to be true.

When the data or EVIDENCE which is used to calculate that probability is itself quantified then the probability can be expressed numerically as a number between 0 (representing impossible) and 1 (representing absolute certainty).

For example, consider the following table which represents evidence gathered about each of the dwarfs in Snow White:

	Dwarf 1	Dwarf 2	Dwarf 3	Dwarf 4	Dwarf 5	Dwarf 6	Dwarf 7
Has a beard			yes	yes		yes	yes
Smokes a pipe		yes	yes			yes	

The probability that any dwarf drawn at random from this set has a beard can be expressed as 4/7 and the probability that any dwarf drawn at random from the set smokes a pipe can be expressed as 3/7. Similarly the probability that a random dwarf doesn't have a beard is 3/7 and the probability that a dwarf, drawn at random, doesn't smoke a pipe is 4/7. So it is more probable than not that a random dwarf will have a beard.

It is not only possible to assign a numerical value to the probability of individual claims when there is quantified data to draw on, as in the examples above, but it is also further possible to calculate the probability of compound claims and conditional claims using the same data. For example, to calculate the probability of the compound claim that a random dwarf will either have a beard or smoke a pipe we add up the number of dwarfs with a beard and the number of dwarfs with a pipe and subtract from that sum (so as to avoid double counting) the number of dwarfs with both beards and pipes and the number left over divided by the total number of dwarfs will be the probability of the claim. In the present case that is 4+3 − 2 over 7 = 5/7. The formula for this calculation is expressed as:

pr (has a beard or smokes a pipe) = pr (has a beard) + pr (smokes a pipe) − pr (has a beard and smokes a pipe).

Or again if one wants to know the probability of a dwarf smoking a pipe given that the dwarf drawn has a beard then this too can be calculated from the data set. There are four dwarfs who have a beard in total and of these, two smoke a pipe so the probability of the conditional claim must be 2/4 from which one can infer that having drawn a dwarf with a beard, it is equally likely that he smokes as pipe as not. The formula for this calculation is expressed as:

pr (smokes a pipe/given he has a beard) = pr (smokes a pipe and has a beard) / pr (has a beard).

The mathematics for calculating probabilities using formulae such as those illustrated above is well established and largely uncontentious. However well-defined the mathematical procedures for calculating numerical probabilities, there remain other problems both practical and theoretical. The practical problems centre on identifying the relevant and appropriate data sets or evidence bases from which to calculate the probabilities in the first place. The probabilities about random dwarfs smoking pipes and having beards could and would change depending upon which groups of dwarfs one collected information on. The theoretical problems relate to the correct interpretation of the meaning of the numbers in the probability claims. Some philosophers, especially those influenced by developments in physics, have interpreted mathematical probabilities as objective features of the world which obtain irrespective of our opinions, beliefs or knowledge. This objectivist interpretation of probability claims has been defended by Karl Popper and more recently by D. H. Mellor. Other philosophers have interpreted mathematical probabilities as subjective features of the world which depend upon the evidence which happens to be available to us while developing our theories and making our predictions. This view of probability claims was defended by Maynard Keynes. The second of these problems is of no direct concern to Critical Thinking but is part of the subject matter of PHILOSOPHY. However, the first practical problem is of interest to critical thinkers who, while not in a position to question the use of mathematics in calculating numerical probabilities, can and should be sensitive to questions about the validity and relevance of the database or reference set which is used to generate these numbers.

However, not all probability claims involve assigning a number between 1 and 0 to a claim. This is true only of those sciences and practices (such as the work of actuaries) which develop comprehensive and detailed quantified databases. In much everyday reasoning and argumentation of the kind which makes up the subject matter of CRITICAL THINKING no such databases are known or presupposed. Nevertheless claims about the probability of claims are made. These claims have the same meaning as numerical probability claims; they mean that the claim which is said to be probable is likely to be true. To support this claim it is sufficient to show that there are plausible reasons and evidence which can be adduced in favour of the claim and that reasons and evidence adduced in favour of its opposite are either weak or flawed. Moreover, as with numerical probability non-numerical probability comes in degrees. It is perfectly possible to rank claims in terms of their relative likelihood of being true without this necessarily implying or requiring that we assign numbers to these different claims. All that is required for a relative ranking of claims with respect to their relative probabilities is that one can discriminate between their supporting arguments in terms of their degrees of STRENGTH AND WEAKNESS. In other words, this claim is supported by a stronger argument than that claim which in turn is supported by a stronger argument than some other claim means that the three claims can legitimately be ranked as more or less probable than each other without it being possible to assign a numerical measure to their probability. This non-numerical employment of probability is common in legal reasoning and ETHICAL REASONING and is integral to Critical Thinking.

Probability is not to be confused with PLAUSIBILITY. A claim is plausible when it is consistent with our knowledge and understanding of the facts. It is thus worthy of serious consideration and not to be rejected out of hand. Plausibility can come in degrees; some claims have a better degree of fit with our background knowledge and understanding than other claims. Nevertheless asserting that a claim is very plausible (has a high level of fit with our other beliefs) falls short of asserting that it is likely to be true. For a claim to be likely to be true there has to be some evidence in its favour. But a claim can be plausible without there being any evidence in its favour. For example, it is plausible to think that I will win the lottery but that does not mean it is probable; in fact it is highly improbable.

To sum up, probability is the likelihood of being true. In some cases, where there is quantified data, it is possible to assign a numerical measure to probability and in such cases there is a well-established branch of mathematics for calculating numerical probabilities. Critical Thinking does not lay claim to any specialist expertise in evaluating mathematical probabilities but the critical thinker is required to have a basic understanding of these calculations and should be sensitive to difficulties that can arise in applying them as a result of selecting inappropriate databases. In much everyday reasoning, especially in law courts, it is not possible to assign numbers to probability claims. Nevertheless such claims are perfectly reasonable and intelligible and are to be supported by comparing the relative strengths and weaknesses of the different arguments offered in support of such claims. The critical evaluation of these claims can fall within Critical Thinking.

See also: PLAUSIBILITY and STRENGTH AND WEAKNESS IN ARGUMENT.

Further reading

Hacking, I. (2001), *An Introduction to Probability and Inductive Logic*. Cambridge: Cambridge University Press.

Mellor, D. H. (2005), *Probability: A Philosophical Introduction*. London: Routledge.

Toulmin, S. (2003), *The Uses of Argument*, updated edn. Cambridge: Cambridge University Press.

Problem solving

generic term for tasks and activities where a goal of some sort is set but the means of getting there is not immediately clear and requires careful thought and application.

Problem solving, like Critical Thinking, is a higher order thinking skill, and involves a variety of sub-skills, with problem-solving activity tending to involve a sequence of processes.

In contrast to Critical Thinking, problem solving tends to be more specifically goal oriented.

Problem solving usually involves the solver overcoming barriers between the given state and the desired goal or state. One barrier is that neither the solution to the problem, nor the means of obtaining it, is self-evident, and hence requires of the solver more than just routine skills. Thus, 'Multiply 4,675 by 9,784' should not require problem solving, since, although it may not be easy and may take skill to reach the answer (assuming no calculator), you have been told exactly what you need to do. The following will require some problem solving in terms of identifying the relevant information and working out the strategy required to reach the solution:

Lenton Cars hire out cars at a cost of £50.00 per day if the number of miles travelled is less than 80. There is an extra charge of £1.00 for every mile travelled over 80 miles. Dunford Hire charge £60.00 per day for taking the car out and then 50 p for every mile travelled.

For how many miles travelled would the cost of hiring a car be the same for both hire companies?

Problem solving has been conceptualized in a wide range of contexts ranging from political decision making, international relations, business and management to mathematics, electronics, information technology and game playing. In common to all these conceptualizations, it is probably true to say that good problem solving can be characterized as an efficient interaction between the solver and the requirements of the task, whether those requirements are numerical, social, societal etc.

Problem Solving is generally thought of as distinct from Critical Thinking, though highly related. Although they share some common reasoning skills (such as SYNTHESIS, judging RELEVANCE and SIGNIFICANCE), the techniques for arriving at a correct solution in problem solving are often different from Critical Thinking – for example, trial and error, insight, lateral thinking and abstraction.

Although a peripheral term to the discipline of Critical Thinking, the connection between problem solving and Critical Thinking is nevertheless significant in that they have historically often been tested alongside one another in thinking skills assessments.

See also: SCIENTIFIC REASONING.

Proof, standards of

To prove: to establish that something must be the case; proof: the justification used to do this.

Standards of proof: the degree of justification required to establish that something is indeed the case in a particular context.

In mathematics, a proof is a means of showing that the answer is correct – that it must be correct – that if you follow the reasoning you will see that the answer has been established with (objective) certainty.

Problems come once the word leaves its strict mathematical usage. In everyday life, 'prove' and 'proof' tend to mean give good/ strong evidence. This wider sense of 'proof' is generally incorrect and/ or largely rhetorical.

Describing evidence as 'proof' implies that there is no longer any doubt, yet this is seldom the case. Evidence which one person sees as incontrovertible, may not be viewed that way by another.

For this reason, different standards of proof apply in different contexts. The best known is the standard used in making a decision in a court of law, where juries are asked to consider whether or not their verdict can be established 'beyond reasonable doubt'. Thus there may still remain logical or hypothetical possibilities that the verdict is wrong, yet such considerations are not deemed reasonable doubt.

Scientific proof is a controversial area, since there is much debate about the extent to which a scientific theory can ever be established through experiment, the reason being that scientific theories are general laws about how the world works, and experiments only ever give *particular* confirmations of theories. Furthermore, these confirmations could be erroneous due to errors with the experiment itself or further theoretical assumptions that the scientist has made in order to generate his or her results or to interpret them the way they have done – see, SCIENTIFIC REASONING. Yet the stamp 'scientifically proven' carries a lot of persuasive weight, and is therefore sometimes exploited, for example, in advertising.

As a general rule, the word 'proof' is best avoided in Critical Thinking. Claiming that your argument 'proves' something almost always makes it vulnerable to criticism and usually refutation. Strictly speaking, the only real proof is deductive proof. Inductive grounds can never establish a conclusion with absolute (objective) certainty. Some philosophers, notably David Hume, argue that there are not even such things as inductive grounds at all – that they provide *no* JUSTIFICATION for beliefs. In Critical Thinking we tend to work with the more common sense view that inductive evidence does give more or less justification, which can even get very close to certainty for all intents and purposes. For example, it seems reasonable to believe that you are justified with near certainty that the sun will rise tomorrow, or that the next time you get a glass of water from your tap it will not contain lethal doses of odourless, colourless poison that will instantly kill you. However, in neither case could you prove that your belief was correct; the only way to know for certain would be to wait and find out. (You might think that, in the case of the sun, you could prove it by referring to the laws of nature and the models of the solar system; but how could you prove that these laws were going to carry on as they have worked up till now into the future? If someone said that it was a genuine possibility that the laws of nature were going to change at midnight tonight, there is no way of proving that they were wrong. You would have to wait until midnight!)

See also: TRUTH, . . . SUBJECTIVE, OBJECTIVE, CERTAINTY and SCIENTIFIC REASONING.

Reason/evidence

REASON: *any claim presented in support of a conclusion (i.e. reason for), or any claim offered as an explanation for a given fact (i.e. reason why).*

EVIDENCE: *information that is a ground for belief, and/or that can establish the truth or falsity of claims.*

Reasons in arguments can include statements of opinion, items claimed to be common knowledge, VALUE JUDGEMENTS, items of evidence, claims about causal relationships and ethical PRINCIPLES. Thus a statement of a piece of evidence can be a reason, though not all reasons are items of evidence.

In the following argument, there is evidence, together with other reasons:

> Researchers investigating the effects of calorie intake on memory asked a group of 60 year-old volunteers to eat 30% fewer calories than normal every day for three months. The ability to remember a list of words was tested before and after this three month period. Their scores in the test were 20% higher after the period of dieting, and were higher than the scores of the average 30-year-old. It is probably true that people in developed countries consume more calories than they need. So it would be sensible for all 60-year-olds in developed countries to reduce their calorie intake. After all, we are all aware that memory deteriorates as we grow old.

The evidence is described in the first three sentences, and these three sentences are all reasons for the conclusion which appears in the penultimate sentence. The other two sentences are reasons and are presented as common knowledge – 'probably true that' and 'we are all aware that' – rather than as items of evidence, nor is any evidence offered to support these claims.

See also: EVIDENCE, REASON and PREMISE.

Reasoning

goal-orientated thinking which moves towards its goal through reflection on reasons.

Reasoning is a form of thinking. But not all thinking is reasoning. What distinguishes reasoning from other forms of thinking such as day dreaming, wishful thinking or fantasy is that it is purposeful thinking subject to the guidance and direction of REASONS. The purpose may be to find an answer to a question or a solution to a problem or even to formulate the right question to ask in the first place. But in each case reasoning is an activity which aims at an end. It is a normative activity, guided by reasons, which means that it is possible to go wrong in reasoning and make mistakes. It is an activity which can be assessed in terms of how well or how badly it is done. It is subject not only to minimal standards of correctness, (mistake, no mistake), but also to standards of excellence which come in degrees. In this sense reasoning is not like a purely natural process such as rusting or erosion. There can be no mistakes in rusting and erosion is not something which can be done well or badly.

The thinking which constitutes reasoning informs most, if not all, purposive human activities that are subject to norms. Thus playing chess, designing a house, planning a road system, drawing up a timetable, seeking a cure for cancer are all activities which involve reasoning. They are not to be thought of as forms of purposive, norm governed, activity distinct from reasoning but rather as several instances or examples of reasoning.

Reasoning is not limited to ARGUMENT but it is central to argument. Argument can be defined as 'reason giving for the purpose of persuasion'. Analysing the argument elements in a passage is itself an exercise of reasoning. Evaluating the strength or weakness of an argument is an exercise of reasoning. Developing and originating new arguments is a paradigm of reasoning. In short, understanding, evaluating and creating arguments all involve reasoning. Hence it is rightly and commonly asserted that 'human reasoning "finds expression" in argument' and again that 'a particular argument is a piece of reasoning'. CRITICAL THINKING as a discipline is almost wholly concerned with developing and educating reasoning in the context of developing, understanding and evaluating arguments. Thus PROBLEM SOLVING is not normally conceived of as part of Critical Thinking and is normally subsumed under what are sometimes called 'Wider Thinking Skills'. These though not part of Critical Thinking as traditionally conceived do nevertheless involve reasoning, that is, purposive thinking directed and led by reasons.

See also: ARGUMENT, INFORMAL LOGIC, LOGIC, REASONS and PROBLEM SOLVING.

Further reading

Finocchiaro, M. (2005), *Arguments about Arguments: Systematic, Critical and Historical Essays in Logical Theory.* Cambridge: Cambridge University Press.

Reasons

claims presented in support of a conclusion (i.e. reason for), or offered as an
explanation for a given fact (i.e. reason why).

It is helpful to draw a distinction between 'reasons for' and 'reasons why'.
Within the context of an ARGUMENT a reason is always a 'reason for'. The reason
is identified with that element within the argument which supports the CON-
CLUSION. So understood, reasons as argument elements are CLAIMS which make
it reasonable for someone to accept the conclusion.

However, in addition to 'reasons for' there are also 'reasons why'. A 'reason why' does *not* purport to persuade someone to accept a conclusion by
showing that the conclusion is reasonable (= supported by reason). Rather a
'reason why' is a claim which purports to explain why some established fact
actually obtains. There is no element of persuasion present and the reason
does not function as a rational persuader offering support for a claim yet to
be accepted by all. The reason explains an established fact, or what is taken
for such, by seeking to show that the given fact fits with our understanding
of how things work.

The difference between these two cases can be simply illustrated by the following two examples:

1. We need to build more prisons because prisons are overcrowded.
2. Prisons are overcrowded because too many prison sentences are being
   given out and too few prisons are being built.

Sentence 1 is a very simple argument composed of one conclusion and one
reason. The aim of the argument is to persuade us that we need to build
more prisons. The reason for this conclusion, which purports to show that it
is a reasonable one to believe, is 'prisons are overcrowded'. This claim clearly
functions as a 'reason for' believing 'we need to build more prisons'.

Sentence 2 is an EXPLANATION. It is not an argument. That prisons are overcrowded is a claim which is offered as an established fact. It is taken as given.
What follows is meant to explain that fact. The two reasons are not reasons

for believing that but rather reasons which purport to explain the intelligibility of what is already believed and accepted. These are not 'reasons for' but 'reasons why'.

See also: REASONING and ARGUMENT VERSUS EXPLANATION.

Recommendation

a particular kind of claim which asserts what ought to be done for the best; or suggests how things should be. 'Proposal' and 'suggestion' are close in meaning, though 'recommendation' is stronger, more assertive.

In the following short argument, the first sentence is a recommendation; the second is an alleged fact:

> A law should be introduced obliging cyclists to wear helmets. HUnnecessary head injuries cost the national health service, and therefore the taxpayer, millions of pounds.

Recommendations should not be confused across the board with statements of PRINCIPLE, although some statements of principle, especially ethical principle, take the form of recommendations. The main difference between the two is that a principle is meant to apply generally, or universally, whereas a recommendation need not. It can be quite particular, as in the example above.

By contrast, take the following claim, which could be used to reinforce the above argument:

> People should not take unnecessary risks at the expense of others.

Although this does make a recommendation, it is about how people should behave in general, which is why we can say that it also asserts a principle. The same cannot be said about the recommendation to introduce a law about helmets, which is a specific, practical proposal.

See also: CLAIMS and CONCLUSION.

Reductio ad absurdum

the Latin name for a form of argument that proceeds by assuming (supposing) the opposite of the intended conclusion and then showing that this leads to an absurdity or contradiction.

Reductio ad absurdum (RAA, RA or *reductio* for short) is a kind of SUPPOSITIONAL REASONING in that it begins with an assumption and assesses its consequences. Here is a classic example:

> Suppose time travel were possible. If it were, I could theoretically travel back in time in time and murder my own grandparents before they had had any offspring. That would mean that I would never have lived, and so could not have travelled back in time. Therefore time travel is not possible.

This example adheres quite strictly to the form of the *reductio*. The author wishes to show that time travel is *not* possible, so he or she starts by supposing that it *is* possible. Since that would lead to a contradiction – someone being alive (to travel in time) and not being alive – the supposition is false and the desired conclusion true.

The name *reductio ad absurdum* is often used more broadly to describe any argument which challenges a claim on the grounds that it is allegedly implausible or unacceptable. For example:

> Some people believe that everyone, regardless of their qualifications, should be paid a standard hourly rate for the work they do, on the grounds that no one's time or labour is worth any more or less than anyone else's. That would mean a brain-surgeon or high court judge earning the same as someone on the check-out at Tesco. The idea is ridiculous.

It should be stressed that *RAA* is not a form of fallacious reasoning, as the name sometimes leads people to think. It is a valid argument. Formally:

> If from A it follows that both B and not-B, then not-A.

That does not mean that every attempt to use the *reductio* is successful or that its premises can never be challenged. Often it is open to question whether the alleged consequence really is a consequence; or, if it is, whether or not it is really absurd. For example, in the second of the two arguments above, it might be objected that there is nothing *absurd* about paying a judge the same as a check-out person. To a committed socialist it might make perfect sense! However, this would not be a fault in the reasoning, only a challenge to the claims and assumptions being made.

See also: SUPPOSITIONAL REASONING.

Refute

prove that a statement is untrue or that an argument is unsound.

A statement can be refuted by EVIDENCE that shows it to be false. For example, someone's statement in court that they were absent from the scene of crime could be refuted by evidence from a CCTV camera.

A general claim can be refuted by a genuine COUNTER-EXAMPLE. For example, the statement that all Members of Parliament have made unacceptable claims for expenses would be refuted if one Member of Parliament were found who had never claimed any expenses.

The words 'refute' and 'refutation' may be used in relation to SCIENTIFIC REASONING. A scientist may formulate a HYPOTHESIS about a particular phenomenon and test the hypothesis by doing an experiment. For example, in the experiment that aimed to find out whether bodies dropped from a height fall at the same speed (see, entry for EMPIRICAL/EMPIRICISM), the hypothesis was that falling bodies will fall at the same speed, and the prediction would have been 'If these two objects are dropped from the top of the leaning tower of Pisa, they will reach the ground at the same time'. If the two objects had reached the ground at different times, then the hypothesis would have been shown to be false, and it may have been claimed that any theory lying behind this hypothesis had been refuted. However, given the difficulty of ensuring that the conditions of experiments are appropriately controlled, it may be controversial to claim that any such result refutes the underlying theory. (See, SCIENTIFIC REASONING.)

It is incorrect to use the word 'refute' to mean the same as 'deny'. To deny something is to state that it is false; to refute something is to prove that it is false. Politicians who want us to believe that they are morally blameless may say 'I refute the allegation that I have claimed expenses to which I was not entitled'. But this statement in itself is merely a denial of the truth of the allegation. To refute it, the politician would have to provide evidence to prove that it was untrue.

See also: COUNTER-EXAMPLE, EMPIRICAL/EMPIRICISM, EVIDENCE and SCIENTIFIC REASONING.

Relevance

(of evidence or reasons) the characteristic of close connection or appropriateness to a topic or a conclusion.

Relevance is a necessary but not sufficient condition for an item of evidence or a reason to support a conclusion. Judging the relevance of evidence or reasons can be a useful first step in the evaluation of an argument, since any claims irrelevant to the conclusion can be dismissed. However, claims judged to be relevant will need further consideration because a relevant claim can count either for or against a conclusion, or may have insufficient SIGNIFICANCE to give strong support.

See also: SIGNIFICANCE.

Reliability

dependability (of authorities and thereby of evidence).

The term 'reliability' is used in CRITICAL THINKING in its normal sense, referring to the extent to which someone or something can be trusted. In general, EVIDENCE can be regarded as reliable if the person presenting the evidence satisfies the following criteria of reliability for authorities:

- Reputation: is the person known to be generally truthful and trustworthy?
- Absence of VESTED INTEREST: would the person lose something by being truthful, or gain something by deceiving others?

- Relevant experience or EXPERTISE: is the person in the position to have the relevant knowledge?
- Quality of judgement: are there factors which could interfere with the accuracy of the person's judgement? (See, OBSERVATIONS, RELIABILITY OF.)

Reliability of evidence is distinct from PLAUSIBILITY of evidence. A question about the plausibility of a piece of evidence is a question about how likely it is that what is presented could be true or could have happened. Both reliability and plausibility come under the umbrella of CREDIBILITY of evidence.

In relation to evidence which comes from research, the term reliability may be applied in a more technical sense, with the trustworthiness of the outcomes being dependent on consistency. For example, the reliability of a test or measurement instrument refers to whether it would produce the same measures when used again. Similarly, the reliability of a research study refers to the extent to which the study, if conducted again, would yield similar findings.

See also: CREDIBILITY, EXPERTISE, OBSERVATIONS (RELIABILITY OF), PLAUSIBILITY and VESTED INTEREST.

Representative

like, or typical of, others of the same group or kind.

For Critical Thinking, a key way of evaluating EVIDENCE is to determine whether or not it has been gathered from a sample (of participants) that represents the group about whom claims are being made. For example, a recent piece of research claimed that teenagers lie mainly due to fear of punishment. To evaluate this claim, we would want to discover whether the sample of teenagers in the research study were sufficiently similar to teenagers in general. For instance, we would want to know whether they were of a similar age distribution, similar mix of ethnicity and class and similar gender balance to all teenagers (for a more detailed discussion of sampling, see, RESEARCH METHODS). If we found that the sample had comprised 80 per cent females and 20 per cent males, it would not be representative of teenagers in general.

Additionally, where an argument deploys the use of an EXAMPLE to support a claim, evaluating the representativeness of example is important:

> Labradors are very intelligent animals. There is a famous case of Archie the black Labrador, who in 2005, when he could not find his owner at Inverurie railway station, boarded the correct train home and got off at the right stop.

To evaluate the claim (itself a GENERALIZATION) that 'Labradors are very intelligent animals' we would need to determine how *representative* Archie is of all Labradors (as well as decide whether or not Archie's behaviour was an example of intelligent behaviour).

See also: BIAS.

Research methods

techniques for collecting information to test a hypothesis or explore an issue.

There are a great many ways of researching any particular research question or HYPOTHESIS. Broadly, these fall into experimental (e.g. laboratory experiments and field experiments) and non-experimental methods (e.g. questionnaires, polls, observations and interviews).

Researchers should select their method primarily on its suitability for the subject matter or hypothesis being investigated. However, differing methods are associated with differing levels of (scientific) rigour, soundness and bearing on real life. Furthermore, especially in the sphere of social sciences, differing methods may yield differing results. One famous example from the subject area of psychology is illustrative here. In the 1960s and 1970s, a number of psychologists conducted research to investigate helping behaviour in an emergency situation (such as when someone collapses unexpectedly). Many of the early studies, which were laboratory experiments, found that a person was more likely to receive help when there was a single bystander than when there were a number of other bystanders. However, later studies which took place in 'the field' (i.e. a normal, everyday environment) found that the number of bystanders present had no effect upon rates of helping. Questionnaires and interviews about hypothetical emergency situations gave different results (probably mainly because people would not want to admit that they may not want to help someone who had collapsed). This area of research illustrates that different research methods can sometimes yield differing results. Thus, when considering research findings it is often worth evaluating how the choice of method may have influenced the results.

One important aspect of research involving participants is the sample (the number and nature of the participants) and the sampling method (the way in which the participants were selected). The key question is whether the sample of participants, for example in a survey, is REPRESENTATIVE of the population in general, or, more importantly, the population about whom the author is making claims. So, when a recent article claims that a travel agent's survey tells us that '26 per cent of Brits keep all the postcards they receive' the author of this claim has made a GENERALIZATION from a *sample* of 'Brits', to *all* 'Brits' (as it would be unfeasible to ask every single member of that population).

But, to evaluate this claim, we would want to know the *size* of the sample in each case (e.g. how many Brits were surveyed) and whether or not the sample is representative of that population in terms of, say, gender, ethnicity, socio-economic background, age and geographic location. Clearly, a large sample (e.g. several thousand people) which has been carefully selected to represent British people gives much more CREDIBILITY to the claim than a small sample of 20 people who just happened to be in the same place as a researcher conducting his/her survey. Good research tends to employ quite sophisticated and time-consuming sampling techniques to increase the representativeness (and, hence, generalizability) of their results. These techniques include 'random sampling' (ensuring each person in the target population has equal chance of being selected to participate in the research) or 'stratified sampling' (ensuring set proportions of the sample have been randomly selected from the relevant sectors of the population).

See also: GENERALIZATION and SCIENTIFIC REASONING.

Restricting the options

See: FALSE DICHOTOMY.

Reverse causation

the flaw of assuming the wrong causal direction in a putative causal relationship.

In most everyday cases of causal attribution it is not difficult to distinguish between cause and effect because the cause typically precedes its effect. Thus in the following examples there is no possibility of confusion:

- Throwing the match onto the haystack caused the barn to burn down.
- The assassination of the Archduke Franz Ferdinand caused the outbreak of the First World War.
- The stabbing was the cause of death.
- Hitting the iceberg was the cause of the Titanic sinking.

In each case the factor or event identified as causally efficacious precedes its effect in time and this is a SUFFICIENT CONDITION when present to distinguish cause from effect. For no one is ever tempted to think that the haystack burning down at 11 a.m. was the cause of the match being thrown two hours earlier at 9 a.m. or the sinking of the Titanic at 3 a.m. was the cause of it hitting the iceberg six hours earlier. In everyday cases of ordinary causality (what philosophers call efficient causality) it is never the case that an effect precedes its cause. So it is impossible to confuse them in such cases.

However, there are cases of causality where CAUSE AND EFFECT are simultaneous. In such cases, temporal priority cannot be used as a criterion to distinguish the cause from the effect. Here are some possible candidates for exemplifying the flaw of reverse causation:

- Increasing secularization in the United Kingdom over the last 50 years is the cause of changing moral standards.
- The increasing tendency for teenagers to carry knives is the cause of the growth in knife crime.
- Frequent and serious quarrels between spouses are the cause of behavioural problems in their children.

In each of the three examples above, it is possible that there is a causal link between the associated or CORRELATED pairs. Of course a critical thinker would also need to consider among other things:

- whether the pairs are mere constant conjunctions, associated but not causally linked at all
- whether the pairs are causally linked but as joint effects of some deeper unidentified cause
- whether the pairs are causally linked as cause and effect but not as the cause and its effect but only as one contributory cause out of many causes acting together.

However, even if for present purposes we assume that there is a causal link between the terms there still remains unresolved the question regarding the direction of causation. It is possible that quarrels between couples cause behavioural problems in their children but it is equally possible that behavioural problems in their children is the cause of their quarrels. It is further possible that there is a causal loop and each is caused by and causes the other. The same possibilities are identifiable for the other examples and many others like them.

There are no methods which can be specified in advance for determining the direction of causation where the cause and effect take place at the same time. Nevertheless a critical thinker presented with such claims should be guided by simple rules constitutive of good thinking such as:

- identify the full range of alternative EXPLANATIONS including no causal link just association, joint effects of some other underlying cause, not the cause but one contributory cause, causal loop and direction of causation can be reversed
- rank the alternatives in terms of their relative PLAUSIBILITY using ANALOGIES from better understood but similar cases
- seek out EVIDENCE to eliminate some possibilities and confirm others
- be open to the possibility that it might not be possible to reach a definite CONCLUSION in such cases until further evidence comes in.

See also: FLAW, INFORMAL FALLACY, POST HOC and CAUSE AND EFFECT.

Further Reading

Mackie, J. L. (2003), *The Cement of the Universe: A Study in Causation.* Oxford: Oxford University Press.

Rhetorical language

language that uses forceful words or expressions in order to persuade.

The word 'rhetoric' has a specialized meaning, that is, the study of the technique of using language effectively. It is also used to refer to speech or writing which is intended to be persuasive, sometimes with the connotation of sounding important while lacking meaning.

When the term 'rhetorical language' is used in the sphere of CRITICAL THINKING, it generally means *language that aims to persuade by means of style or strong words rather than sound reasoning or argument.*

Rhetorical language may use strongly emotive terms to get readers or hearers to agree with the point being made. For example, politicians may describe an opponent's view as 'fatuous', or describe a policy as a '*disgraceful* waste of the money which the government *extracts* from *hard-working* taxpayers'. The words in italics in the last phrase are intended to persuade hearers or readers that the policy is much more objectionable than they may have thought. A more neutral phrase – 'a waste of the money which the government gets from taxpayers' – is a criticism of the policy, without also being an attempt to attack the reputation of the government.

This is not to say that rhetorical language should never be used in reasoning; it can make dull-sounding arguments more interesting to read, and does not necessarily mask their important message. But critical thinkers need to be alert to its use when listening to or reading others' arguments, and need to be able to separate the reasoning from the rhetoric.

Some INFORMAL FALLACIES are described as rhetorical devices, for example, FALSE DICHOTOMY and STRAW MAN.

Another rhetorical device, persuasive DEFINITION, defines a term in such a way as to invite approval or disapproval. For example, in a debate about whether abortion is morally acceptable, defining abortion as 'murder' is an attempt to persuade hearers that abortion is wrong, and could also be said to commit the fallacy of BEGGING THE QUESTION.

See also: APPEALS, BEGGING THE QUESTION, FALSE DICHOTOMY and PERSUASIVE LANGUAGE.

Scepticism (also spelt skepticism)

an inclination or tendency to doubt. A sceptic is a person who is disposed to doubt what others might accept.

A degree of active scepticism is an essential ingredient of Critical Thinking. It is the opposite of passive acceptance, that is, believing everything one reads or hears. For example, when looking at an argument based on evidence, it is important to ask questions such as:

- Is the source reliable?
- Might the author have a vested interest in the outcome and therefore have been selective with the data?
- Is the person giving 'expert' opinion really qualified to do so?

These are *sceptical* questions.

In many disciplines scepticism has been used as a methodology, intended to remove all possibility of error. The method is often referred to as 'philosophical scepticism'. The basic idea is to begin by doubting everything that cannot be known with certainty and to proceed from there by accepting only what can be validly inferred from what is known with certainty. The trouble with philosophical scepticism is that it is very difficult to find anything which cannot be doubted to some degree. Indeed one sceptical view is that nothing can be known, except perhaps one's own existence. This was the position taken by the French philosopher Rene Descartes, who rejected everything except the certainty that he was thinking – which he had to do in order to doubt. Hence one of the shortest and most famous arguments in history – *Cogito ergo sum* – I think therefore I am.

In the context of Critical Thinking, scepticism should obviously not be taken to such extremes. Refusing to believe anything as a matter of course is no more critical than accepting everything. A critical approach means weighing up the grounds for and against a claim or belief and then making a balanced and informed judgement.

Scepticism should also not stray into *cynicism*. A cynic is someone who assumes the worst in people, or makes a habit of being negative. A fair-minded sceptic might say that because a particular statement or argument has come from a political party it may be biased, and treat its claim with caution. A cynic might say, 'No politician ever tells the truth unless it makes them rich or gets them votes. Don't believe a word of it'.

'FAIR-MINDED sceptic' would be a good way to describe an effective critical thinker.

See also: PROOF, STANDARDS OF.

Scientific reasoning

reasoning from careful observation and experiment, especially for the purposes of explaining phenomena, formulating general laws and testing hypotheses.

Traditionally, scientific reasoning (or scientific method) has been characterized as a series of carefully executed steps or stages:

1. observation and experiment
2. generalization based on inductive reasoning
3. formulating HYPOTHESES / theories
4. testing hypotheses with the aim of verifying them
5. proof (or disproof).

Consider the following example of reasoning about the ocean tides. Observers (e.g. sailors) notice the rise and fall of water along the coast, and draw general conclusions about the patterns they follow. Some notice a connection with the changing positions of the moon and sun, and advance the hypothesis that the sun and moon cause (or causally explain) tidal motion. They put the hypothesis to the test by predicting high and low tides in relation to the lunar–solar calendar, and discover that their predictions (if carefully calculated) are always correct and take this to be the verification / proof.

Certainly, this is not the proof, and the hypothesis is only partially correct. The same observations and predictions could have been used to 'prove' that the tides cause (or explain) the motions of the sun and moon, or that tides and planetary motions have a common cause – as later scientists claimed.

Scientific method does not guarantee absolute truth or knowledge, as the history of science has shown over and over again. Nonetheless it is a form of reasoning which is hugely successful (e.g. in the advance of technology) and on which we rightly place great reliance.

However, some philosophers (most notably Karl Popper) have questioned the traditional account, claiming instead that science proceeds (and/or *should* proceed) by efforts to falsify rather than verify hypotheses. A good scientific theory is one which *could* be falsified – if predictions made on the strength of it turn out to be wrong – but which has so far resisted falsification. Likewise good science is the strenuous testing of hypotheses by *attempting* to falsify them. Popper and his supporters are especially sceptical about the role of INDUCTION. The problem with induction is that no matter how many millions of observations are made, or experiments conducted, which confirm a hypothesis, there is always the possibility that the next one (or some future one) might *disconfirm* it. In practice this problem is aggravated by the danger of 'confirmation bias', that is, the natural tendency of a researcher to concentrate on observations and experiments which favour a chosen hypothesis, and ignore or explain away those that might threaten it.

Some understanding of these issues is of obvious relevance in Critical Thinking. This is not because science itself has any special importance in Critical Thinking, but because many of the methods of reasoning used in science are found in arguments generally, whatever the subject matter. A good critical thinker will approach the evaluation of argument with the same kind of scepticism and rigour as a good scientist approaches the evaluation of scientific theories.

See also: HYPOTHESIS, (ARGUMENT AND) EXPLANATION, INDUCTION and ABDUCTION.

Significance

the importance and/or implications of evidence, claims or events in relation to an issue under consideration.

In Critical Thinking the term 'significant' may be applied to reasons offered for a conclusion, or to EVIDENCE or claims from which a conclusion may be drawn.

For example, evidence that passive smoking can cause lung cancer is significant in relation to the question as to whether a law against smoking in public places is justifiable. Its significance lies both in its importance as evidence that smoking can cause serious harm to non-smokers and in its implication that a law against smoking in public places can help protect non-smokers from such harm.

In the field of statistics, 'significance' has a related, though more precise and technical meaning. Statistical significance indicates that the probability of, say, a result in an experiment occurring by chance alone, is below a certain agreed level (often 5 per cent).

See also: RELEVANCE.

Skill(s)

an ability, acquired through practice and training, exercised in the service of some other end, and whose exercise can be appraised in terms of how well or how badly it is done.

Skills are typically internal to and subordinate to a craft or trade. Thus a carpenter will have one set of skills relative to the making of wooden furniture, a chef will possess a different set of skills relative to the making of an appetizing meal and a footballer will possess yet another set of skills relative to the aim of wining football matches. Generalizing from these paradigm cases, it is possible to identify five central characteristics of a skill:

1. They are acquired through practice and training.

They no doubt presuppose innate capacities but are normally thought of as additional to them rather than being identifiable with them. Thus my ability to hear sounds is not in itself a skill but if that ability is developed and trained to recognize and distinguish different bird sounds that may be classified as a skill.

2. They can be exercised with varying degrees of success.

Footballers, carpenters and violinists differ in their skilfulness; some footballers are more skilful than others.

3. They are exercised on something else.

Carpenters exercise their skills on wood, footballers exercise their skills on the ball and violinists exercise their skills on the violin itself.

4. They are exercised in and through something else.

Carpenters use their hands and a lathe, violinists use their fingers and a bow and footballers use their feet. But in each case an instrument or tool of some sort is employed, more or less skilfully, to produce the desired effect.

5. They are exercised in the service of a craft or activity whose goal they help to realize.

The skills of the carpenter are pointless apart from the aim of producing furniture; the skills of the footballer make no sense apart from the aim of wining football matches and the skills of the virtuoso violinist are meaningless apart from the aim of producing music.

A strong claim on behalf of these five characteristics would be that they are jointly necessary and sufficient for anything to count as a skill. A weaker claim would be that the concept of a skill is, in the sense made familiar by Wittgenstein, a 'family resemblance' concept and that although all five characteristics are present in our central examples it may be that the term can be applied to other abilities which share some of these characteristics but not all.

The term is now widely used within education to cover social skills, language skills, emotional skills and even thinking skills. The appeal of the term within educational circles is in part because skills are not innate but acquired. Insofar as they are acquired through practice and example they can be taught and, albeit with varying degrees of success, taught to almost anyone. Skills are intrinsically democratic and egalitarian insofar as they build on and add to, in non-mysterious ways, natural human capacities. They further appeal because of their practicality and instrumentality. They bestow upon their possessors an ability to get things done and therefore render their possessor useful, to some degree, and relative to, some specifiable end. However, the term is now used so widely and so uncritically that it cannot simply be assumed without further argument that all these things referred to as skills are in fact skills. Moreover even if these activities, speaking, thinking and socially interacting, do involve skills it cannot be assumed that skills constitute the whole or even the most significant part of these activities.

Critical Thinking skills are thought of as those skills underpinning the reasoning which is primarily present in analysing, evaluating and constructing arguments. The taxonomy of Critical Thinking skills in Black et al. (2008) identifies over twenty sub-skills or processes which fall under these three broader categories. However, the identification of these processes or abilities with skills, is not unproblematic or without controversy. The first concern is that skills as instrumental means to execute our ends are value neutral. The same skill can be used for good and bad purposes alike. The skill which enables the footballer to score the wining penalty is the same skill which will enable him or her, if he or she is corrupt and takes a bribe, to deliberately miss the penalty. Similarly the skill of the violinist which can be used to produce the right notes can be equally used to produce the wrong notes if he or she wants to do that. So Critical Thinking cannot simply be a matter of skill. A critical thinker will also require virtuous dispositions to care about and value certain ends. Otherwise education in thinking skills may simply develop craftiness, cunning, cleverness and guile so that one can produce well-crafted arguments in defence of falsehoods and provide densely argued justifications for criminal acts. No doubt such skills, in the absence of virtuous dispositions, will confer upon their possessor both utility and marketable value but it cannot be the goal of education to produce such people.

The second concern is more fundamental and challenges the very identification of Critical Thinking abilities with skills. There is, indeed, a prima facie case for this identification. Nevertheless, there are also arguments against this assimilation. There is a distinction to be drawn between doings which are transitive and doings which are intransitive. An example of the former is carving wood into a peg and an example of the latter is listening to music. With action which is transitive we act upon something else and change it. With action which is intransitive we do not act upon something else so as to change its position or shape or constitution. The music is not changed by our listening to it but stays the same even though listening is something we do and something we can do well or badly. By contrast the wood is changed by our action as it is shaped into a peg. Now understanding an argument is more like listening to music than carving wood into a peg. It is something which we can indeed do well or badly and indeed learn to do well; but crucially, as with listening to music, the action is intransitive; in understanding an argument we do not change it in anyway. Skills, at least in all the paradigm cases, are properly thought of as instrumental means in the service of our transitive deeds. They enable us to manipulate things to serve our ends. If this is correct then intransitive actions cannot involve skills in any literal sense of the term. In which case the abilities which make up Critical Thinking and which the discipline aims to foster and develop are not really skills at all. Clearly it is sufficient to note here the existence of this debate. The debate itself is ongoing, as is the debate about the full educational implications of these different views.

See also: VIRTUE and CRITICAL THINKING.

Further reading

Black, B., Chislett, J., Thomson, A., Thwaites, G., and Thwaites, J. (2008), 'Critical Thinking – A Definition and Taxonomy for Cambridge Assessment'. Research Matters 6, A Cambridge Assessment publication.

Hart, W. A. (1978), 'Against Skills'. *Oxford Review of Education*, 4(2), 205–16.

Lipman, M. (2003), *Thinking in Education*, 2nd edn. Cambridge: Cambridge University Press.

McGuinness, C. (1999), *From Thinking Skills to Thinking Classrooms: A Review and Evaluation of Approaches for Developing Pupils' Thinking*. London: Department for Education and Employment.

Zagzebski, L. T. (1996), *Virtues of the Mind: An Inquiry into the Nature of Virtue and the Ethical Foundations of Knowledge*. Cambridge: Cambridge University Press.

Slippery slope

fallacious hypothetical reasoning.

The slippery slope, in its most common and simplest form, is just a hypothetical syllogism made up of lots of weak links. A hypothetical syllogism has the form of:

- If A then B.
- If B then C.
- If C then D.

- If D then E.
- Therefore if A then E.

Obviously as it stands such a CHAIN OF REASONING is deductively VALID. However, whether it is sound reasoning or not will depend on the degree of PROBABILITY attaching to each of the links. If there is good supporting evidence making each of the links highly probable then the whole can be accepted as good hypothetical reasoning. But not all HYPOTHETICAL REASONING of this form is good, sound reasoning. Thus, a mother in an effort to persuade her son of the need to eat greens might argue:

- If you don't eat your greens then you will not grow up big and strong.
- If you don't grow up big and strong you will not get a job.
- If you don't get a job then you will turn to crime.
- If you turn to crime you will end up in prison for life.
- Therefore if you don't eat your greens you will end up in prison for life.

Clearly each link in this chain of reasoning is very weak and multiplying the number of weak links in the chain only serves to weaken the support for the final conclusion even further. Consequently, the CONCLUSION is overblown and incredible in relation to the REASONING offered in its support. The ARGUMENT is indeed ridiculously bad.

The above account suffices to show that the causal slippery slope clearly fits the familiar, current definition of INFORMAL FALLACY as deficient or FLAWED argument with easily recognizable form. For it is an argument form characterized by a sweeping conclusion and a weak chain of less than adequate REASONS. However, it is also possible to provide a deeper ANALYSIS of the fallacy which shows that it further satisfies the traditional criteria of an informal fallacy furnished by Aristotle. According to the traditional account, offered by Aristotle, a fallacy should be both deceptive in some way and involve an actual mistake in reasoning. Both conditions can be shown to obtain when the slippery slope fallacy is investigated in more detail.

A brief sketch of such an analysis may suffice here. Regarding the first condition, it should be sufficient to note that the slippery slope fallacy is deductively VALID. It is deductively valid because it is an instance of the hypothetical syllogism. Hence the validity of the argument form may be sufficient, in many cases, though not in all, to deceive the unsuspecting into accepting its conclusion. Regarding the second condition it will be helpful to compare the slippery slope with the classical argument form, REDUCTIO AD ABSURDUM. The reductio is a hypothetical syllogism whose final conclusion is contradictory and is used in mathematics and logic as a PROOF for rejecting the initial premise which gives rise to it. In effect a reductio reasons to a conclusion whose falsehood is so patent that it succeeds in overturning its own starting point. Now clearly a slippery slope does not set out to be a reductio ad absurdum even though it shares with the reductio the same logical form of the hypothetical syllogism. However, though it does not set out to be a reductio it clearly ends up, despite itself, being exactly that. It ends up as a reductio because it arrives at a conclusion which is so patently false and exaggerated and ridiculous (this is so in the paradigm, stock teaching examples) that this only serves to overturn its own premises. What this shows is that the causal slippery slope is fallacious in the traditional Aristotelian sense of the term. It is not simply an instance of a weak argument but is an instance of a chain of reasoning which actually refutes its own premises quite contrary to the intention of the reasoner. In other words, the slippery slope argument is the same argument form as a classical reductio ad absurdum, only this is not apparent to the author of the reasoning, who thereby succeeds, not in establishing his or her own conclusion, but only in refuting his or her own claims. The mother means to establish that not eating greens has terrible consequences but only succeeds in proving the opposite.

See also: FLAW, INFORMAL FALLACY, HYPOTHETICAL REASONING and SYLLOGISM.

Further reading

Finocchiaro, M. (2005), *Arguments about Arguments: Systematic, Critical and Historical Essays in Logical Theory*. Cambridge: Cambridge University Press.

Sound argument

an argument with true reasons which give conclusive support to its conclusion.

Soundness of argument is not synonymous with VALIDITY of argument. A valid argument is one in which it would not be possible for its reasons to be true and yet its conclusion to be false. However, an argument can be valid even if its reasons are false. All sound arguments are valid; not all valid arguments are sound.

The following two arguments are valid, though the first has true reasons, and the second has false reasons:

1. All insects have only six legs. Spiders have eight legs. So spiders are not insects.

2. All reptiles are furry. Dolphins are reptiles. So dolphins are furry.

Argument 1 is sound as well as valid, because its reasons are true, and its conclusion follows logically from the reasons. Argument 2 is valid but not sound, because its reasons are false.

The above definition of 'sound argument' is the traditional definition from the discipline of formal logic. An argument that is not sound in this strict sense may nevertheless be a good argument, provided that it has true or acceptable reasons which give strong support to its conclusion. Here is an example of such an argument:

> There is wide agreement amongst environmental scientists that irreversible and catastrophic change in our climate is likely to result if the world's level of carbon dioxide emissions is not curbed soon. It is becoming clear to scientists and politicians that international agreement to reduce levels is very difficult to achieve. Thus it would be sensible for scientists to start to explore other possible ways of preventing the Earth's climate from becoming increasingly warmer.

The reasons in this argument (the first two sentences) can be accepted as true, given a report in the *New Scientist* magazine (28 February 2009) that a meeting of politicians and climate scientists in 2008 came to agreement that we are faced with 'potentially catastrophic climate change' and that 'cuts to carbon emissions will likely fall short' of what is needed. The reasons give strong support to the conclusion, because if other ways of preventing warming can be found, the catastrophe may be avoided. But it would not be impossible for the reasons to be true and yet the conclusion false, if, for example, scientists made hasty and dangerous decisions about other solutions to the problem.

In CRITICAL THINKING there is no technical term to describe good arguments such as the above example, and in some texts you may find that the term 'sound' is borrowed from the field of logic, and used to refer to good non-deductive arguments that have true reasons.

See also: EVALUATION, INDUCTION and VALIDITY.

Statistical reasoning

reasoning which focuses upon interpreting statistics and the inferences that may be validly drawn from statistical evidence.

Statistical reasoning, put simply, is reasoning on the basis of statistical evidence and thus shares many characteristics and skills of Critical Thinking in terms of judging RELEVANCE, SUFFICIENCY and SIGNIFICANCE. However, statistical reasoning may also involve an, sometimes quite sophisticated, understanding of statistical concepts and assumptions behind their usage. These may include, among others, probability and chance, MEASURES OF CENTRAL TENDENCY and dispersion, CORRELATION, significance testing, interpretation of graphs and issues around sampling. There is not enough space to discuss or develop all of these aspects in detail, though some examples below may be illuminating.

Statistical reasoning is at the heart of evidence-based decision making in public policy. Decisions about making changes in the education system, whether or not a new drug should be used to treat a certain disorder, the risks of using pesticides – all will have involved some statistical reasoning. At a more private or individual level, statistical reasoning plays some sort of role in deciding whether to avoid certain types of food, take out an insurance policy against redundancy, whether to go through IVF, play the lottery, buy a new car or take an umbrella when going out. As rational human beings, we have to make sense of any statistical information we may be in possession of, such as the vitamin content per 100g of the food, the proportion of people being made redundant in similar job areas in recent months, the percent likelihood of success of IVF given various factors such as age of mother, the percent chance of winning some money, the average number of miles to the gallon etc. As each statistic is a single summary of the available data, good statistical reasoning often involves understanding how that particular statistic is calculated, how it relates to the data as a whole and under what conditions the statistic may be misleading.

Statistical reasoning is not always sound (see, entries for FALLACIES, POST HOC and GENERALIZATION) and further examples are given below to illustrate how common flaws in statistical reasoning can lead to unsubstantiated inferences (and poor decision making):

1. *The gambler's fallacy* – A gambler is betting money on whether the throw of a coin will be heads or tails. The last four throws have been heads. On this basis, the gambler reasons that it must, by now, be time for the coin to fall on tails, and so wagers £100. However, he has made a classic flaw in his reasoning. Each throw of the coin is independent of the previous one and therefore the odds of it being a tail is *still* 50:50.

2. *Ignorance of how sample size affects statistical variation* – A parent in a UK city looks at the school league tables (calculated on proportion of students achieving at or above a level 4 in Key Stage 2 results) and decides to move house to ensure his small child gets into the primary school at the top of the league table in her city. The inference he is making is that this is, and will continue to be, the best school for getting good academic results. However, the league tables do not necessarily support this inference, in particular because they do not communicate the UNCERTAINTY in results. In fact, there is inevitably variation, year on year, in each school due to the nature of the particular class of the children taking the Key Stage exams. The rankings are very volatile essentially because the test results are more a result of the pupils rather than the school or teachers, and each school only has a small number of pupils (e.g. 30 or 60) each year. It might be more helpful to parents if league tables showed the probability that a school in top rank position really is due to the school being the best! Howard Wainer recently noted a number of examples of how such ignorance of sample size affects statistical variation. His examples include:
   a. the mistaken investment in smaller schools on the basis that among high-performing schools there is an unrepresentatively large proportion of smaller schools. Wainer claims this is not because they are genuinely

or consistently better, but because small samples tend to produce more extreme data.

b. An insurance company's tables of the ten safest and least safe US cities for driving – and upon which, presumably, the company used to base their car insurance premiums. These tended to be the cities with relatively small populations, not because, Wainer claims, they are intrinsically safer or more dangerous cities, but just that smaller populations are more likely to be associated with extreme outcomes than larger populations as a statistical artefact.

3. *(Mis)calculating the probability of an event occurring more than once* – A number of women (e.g. Angela Canning and Sally Clark) were convicted, in high-profile cases, of the murder of their small children, who, they had persistently claimed, had died from Sudden Infant Death Syndrome (Cot Death). There was no medical evidence that the children had been murdered. In the case of Sally Clark, the jury was swayed by the 'evidence' presented in court by Sir Roy Meadows that, while the odds of one baby dying from cot death in one home was 1 in 8,500, the probability of two babies dying in one home was 1 in 73 million. However, the statistical reasoning was erroneous. Meadows had calculated the odds of an event happening twice by multiplying the odds of it happening once by itself again: $\frac{1}{8500} \times \frac{1}{8500}$, (in the same way as calculating the probability of getting two sixes on two shakes of dice would be $\frac{1}{6} \times \frac{1}{6}$). The assumption behind this calculation is that the events are entirely independent and unlinked. But, in the case of Clark's two children, cot death is likely related to genetic factors and/or environmental factors and Sally Clark's babies would have shared 50 per cent of their genetic material. Thus, Meadows' statistics were hugely misleading, and the inferences the jury made were not valid. In 2001, the Royal Statistical Society released a document expressing their concern, stating that the figure of 1 in 73 million was statistically invalid. Clark's and Canning's convictions were overturned, in recognition of the faulty statistical reasoning.

4. *Context and significance* – In 1995, the Committee on the Safety of Medicines (CSM) issued advice that doctors should stop prescribing the new generation contraceptive pill. This advice was based upon the statistical evidence that women who took these types of pills were twice as likely to suffer from potentially serious blood clots (venous thromboembolism – VTE) than those who took an older form of the pill. In the wake of media

coverage, there was a 14 per cent drop in prescriptions for the pill. The subsequent increase in abortion rates (especially among teenagers) was blamed on this 'pill scare'. However, the initial advice was based on poor statistical reasoning. While 'twice as likely' sounds like a serious increase, it is still important to look at the overall rate and put it in context in order to judge the SIGNIFICANCE of this change. The incidence of VTE for women taking the newer Pill is 25 per 100,000 women per year; this compares with 15 per 100,000 for women taking the older Pill; and 60 per 100,000 women who develop VTE in pregnancy. Therefore, the increase in risk was still very small – and still less than that for a woman who falls pregnant.

5. *Understanding the mean in the context of the data's distribution* – I am deciding where to go on holiday and warmth is an important criterion. The average (MEAN) temperature for May both in the Canary Islands and Sorrento is 23°C. I infer that I could expect a similar temperature in either the Canaries or Sorrento, and so either destination would meet my criteria. However, this may not be true. That is because we have to take into consideration the *distribution* of temperatures. So, while Sorrento can be quite chilly in the early mornings and evenings in May, and varies quite a lot in terms of year-to-year averages, the Canaries maintain a much more constant daytime temperature.

6. *Confusing low or high probabilities for absolutes* – The weather forecast informs us that there is a low risk of rain today – about 5 per cent. I don't take any wet-weather gear on my long walk and this turns out to be a regrettable mistake when I get rather wet. I had interpreted 5 per cent chance of rain as 'it will not rain' and so the inferences were faulty. Theoretically, on 20 occasions where the Meteorological Office advises of a 5 per cent probability of rain, there will be 19 occasions of no rain and one occasion when it will rain.

Finally, some errors in statistical reasoning may not necessarily be due to a misunderstanding of any statistical concept or concepts, but rather because our statistical reasoning, especially with regard to *risk*, can be unduly influenced by emotional factors (e.g. fear and denial).

Further reading

Wainer, H. (2008), *The Second Watch: Navigating An Uncertain World*. Princeton, NJ: Princeton University Press.

Straw man

the informal fallacy of attributing a weak or inaccurate version of an opponent's argument or viewpoint, which can then very easily be knocked down.

A 'straw man' may be presented in direct response to another argument that has been explicitly put forward, or it may appear when the author anticipates a counter-argument, envisaging the kind of argument the other side *would* give. In this latter case it could be said that the author is 'putting words into the opponent's mouth', resulting in a poor or caricatured version of what they would reasonably be expected to say. In this weakened form, the opposing argument becomes easier to defeat.

Here is an example:

> The government's recommendation for a healthy diet advises consuming five portions of fruit or vegetables a day. However we would soon become bored with eating salad throughout the day and it would hardly provide the energy needed for the busy lifestyle that so many of us have.

The author misrepresents the government's recommendation in that the five portions were intended to be part of a healthy diet, not the whole of it. Other foods could be the energy producers. Moreover, the government recommendation includes more than salad, so the recommended diet need neither be boring nor lacking in energy producing foods. Had the author presented an accurate version of the recommendation, they would have had to produce stronger reasoning in their response.

The straw man fallacy and the AD HOMINEM fallacy are both unjustifiably dismissive of an opponent's position. They differ in that the straw man misrepresents an opponent's argument, whereas an AD HOMINEM flaw attacks the opponent rather than their argument. The following is an example of ad hominem reasoning:

> We shouldn't attempt to follow the government's radical recommendations for a change in diet, since members of the government are hardly the stick insects that they obviously want us to become.

This argument uses abuse against members of the government as a reason to reject their recommendations, rather than dealing with the reasoning supporting their recommendation.

See also: RHETORIC and INFORMAL FALLACIES.

Strength and weakness (of claims and arguments)

semi-technical terms used in the assessment of both claims and arguments.

The best way to explain strength and weakness of claims is by example. Compare these three claims:

1. Alcohol is a deadly poison to be avoided under all circumstances.

This is a strong claim, categorical and emphatic. By contrast, the next two claims are much *weaker*:

2. Alcohol is a toxic substance which should be taken in moderation.
3. Excessive consumption of alcohol can be harmful.

Claims are typically strengthened by the inclusion of terms such as 'all', 'always', 'never', 'must', 'only' and 'under all circumstances'. They are weakened by moderating terms such as 'sometimes', 'can be', 'should', 'on occasions', 'in some respects' and the like.

Strong conclusions require proportionately strong premises to justify them. This is an obvious point, but it is important to bear it in mind when evaluating arguments. A strong *argument* is an argument in which the reasons or premises are themselves strong enough to support the conclusion. If the conclusion is too strong this may result in a weak (inadequate) argument – and *vice versa*. Compare the following two potential conclusions in relation to the three claims above:

4. Out and out prohibition is the only responsible policy.
5. An advertising campaign is needed to discourage alcohol abuse.

Only claim 1offers the strength of support needed to justify a claim like 4.

Claims 2 and 3 are both inadequate grounds for claim 4, but could be offered in support for claim 5, because 5 is a much weaker conclusion.

See also: FALLACY (FORMAL), FALLACY (INFORMAL), FLAW and EVALUATION.

Subjective

See: OBJECTIVE.

Supposition

an assumption that is put forward for consideration. It is not a claim as such because it is not being presented as a fact, nor even as an opinion on the author's part.

When a person makes a supposition he or she does not have to believe it or agree with it or even like it. Indeed, a supposition is often made in the knowledge that it is not true:

Suppose the English Premiership had capped footballers' wages at a level comparable to other skilled professionals in this country – dentists say.

The Premiership has clearly not capped wages. This is clear from the opening word, 'Suppose. . .'. It is a hypothetical situation that is being considered.

Suppositions can also be made about future possibilities that may or may not turn out to be true:

Suppose the English Premiership were to cap footballers wages at a level comparable to other skilled professionals . . .

Even impossibilities can be supposed simply out of interest, to try out ideas or play mind games:

Suppose someone could travel back in time and meet their own younger self. . .!

See also: SUPPOSITIONAL REASONING.

Suppositional reasoning

reasoning which starts with a SUPPOSITION *and proceeds by considering its consequences and drawing a conclusion accordingly.*

Here is an argument that uses a form of suppositional reasoning:

> Suppose the English Premiership were to cap footballers wages at level comparable to other skilled professionals in this country. Unless the other footballing nations set similar limits, the world-class players who play for English clubs would soon disappear to other countries and the standard of football would deteriorate rapidly. On the other hand, more English players would experience premiership competition, and the national side would benefit. Therefore, there would be gains and losses.

The author makes the supposition, weighs the consequences and concludes that a cap on players' wages has pros and cons.

Suppositional reasoning is very common in decision making. Think of someone playing chess, and reasoning:

> If I play the black knight, white can put me in check and could then take my queen with her next move whatever I do. Therefore, I must play a different piece.

See also: HYPOTHETICAL REASONING and REDUCTIO AD ABSURDUM.

Syllogism

is a deductive argument composed of two premises, one conclusion and three terms. The two premises share exactly one term and the conclusion contains the two terms which are not shared.

Standard examples of valid syllogisms include arguments of the following form:

1. All footballers are athletes.
2. All athletes are disciplined.
3. So all footballers are disciplined.

1. No footballers are disciplined.
2. All athletes are disciplined.
3. So no footballers are athletes.

1. All footballers are disciplined.
2. Some athletes are footballers.
3. So some athletes are disciplined.

1. No footballers are disciplined.
2. Some athletes are footballers.
3. So some athletes are not disciplined.

Interest in understanding and codifying the underlying logical form of ARGU-MENTS such as these began with Aristotle. His account of the logical structure of these arguments began with a prior account of the logical form or structure of the statements which make them up. All the statements are analysed by Aristotle as involving two terms, the subject term, which identifies what it is you are talking about, and the predicate term which identifies what it is you say about it. Thus in the claim that footballers are disciplined, the subject term is 'footballers' and the predicate term is 'are disciplined' and the combination of the two terms adds up to the claim that footballers are disciplined. He further noted that all these statements will involve, either explicitly or implicitly, a quantifier expression such as 'all' or 'some' or 'none'. So fully expressed, the claim about footballers being disciplined will either be all footballers are disciplined or some footballers are disciplined or some footballers are not disciplined or no footballers are disciplined.

Aristotle then proceeded to identify and categorize VALID and invalid argument forms for simple arguments of two premises where the premises corresponded to the logical form described above, of subject term, predicate term and quantifiers. These are the arguments now known as syllogisms. He classified these syllogisms by figure and by mood. Classification by figure refers to the possible permutations for the term common to both premises, that is, when the common term is subject in one premise and predicate in a second premise this is classed as 'first figure'; when the common term is predicate in both this is called 'second figure' and when the common term is subject in both this is called 'third figure'. Classification by mood refers to the possible permutations arising out of the possible mutations of the quantifier expressions, whether the terms are qualified by 'all' or 'none' or 'some' or 'some not'.

Aristotle then proceeded to demonstrate that all valid syllogisms could be derived from two fundamental forms of syllogism together with a small number of basic rules of inference. He further proceeded to argue that all arguments of more than two premises, polysyllogisms, could be reduced to sequences of valid syllogisms. In effect, Aristotle was claiming that all valid arguments in natural languages could be expressed as syllogisms and all valid syllogisms could in turn be derived from a few basic forms together with a small number of rules of inference. The reality is more modest. Not all valid arguments in natural language are deductively valid and not all deductively valid arguments are syllogisms. It is a vast oversimplification to say that the logical form of all statements is made up of subject terms and predicates. The most that can be said is that some arguments in natural language are syllogistic in form and for these Aristotle's account of their logical form and behaviour is adequate. Hence Critical Thinking fully accepts Aristotle's analysis of syllogistic arguments as and when they are found in everyday reasoning but rightly rejects his far-fetched claim that such an ANALYSIS is adequate for the understanding and evaluation of all arguments.

See also: LOGIC and INFORMAL LOGIC.

Further reading

Smith, R. (2007), *Aristotle's Logic*. Stanford Encyclopaedia of Philosophy.

Synthesis

the disciplined, creative activity whereby facts and information are organized and interpreted both to produce original solutions to problems and to create and develop new arguments out of materials whose significance and relevance is not fully understood prior to the act of synthesis.

Within Critical Thinking, synthesis is the term given to the construction of new and original ARGUMENTS out of appropriately interpreted and organized EVIDENCE and other raw materials for argument construction. This active and creative process presupposes a prior grasp and understanding of ARGUMENT STRUCTURES, as well as the skills of gathering, interpreting and evaluating evidence. The same active processing of information and evidence, and of argument construction, also underlies practical decision making, resolving ethical DILEMMAS and arriving at reasoned judgements when weighing up evidence on different sides of a question.

Within wider Thinking Skills, synthesis is the term given to the construction of solutions to problems where that activity likewise presupposes prior skills of gathering, interpreting, organizing and evaluating data and information. In each case synthesis is a higher order skill of constructing something new through the transformation of prior material.

See also: CRITICAL THINKING, CREATIVE THINKING and PROBLEM SOLVING.

Truth

conformity with reality.

The question of truth arises for critical thinkers in relation to purportedly factual claims made in reasoning, in particular to reasons given to support conclusions of arguments. Evaluating argument involves both assessing whether reasons are true, and whether, if true, they give support to the conclusion.

Truth is not the same as VALIDITY. Often in everyday conversation the word 'valid' is used to mean 'true', or even 'relevant', and is applied to supposedly factual claims in the same way as is the word 'true'. However, in LOGIC and in CRITICAL THINKING, claims are never described as 'valid'. 'True or false' applies to claims; 'valid or invalid' applies to the relationship between the claims made in the reasons and the claim which is the conclusion of an argument. An ARGUMENT is valid if and only if it would not be possible for its reasons to be true, and yet its conclusion to be false.

See also: EVALUATION, FACT AND OPINION, SOUND ARGUMENT and VALIDITY.

Tu quoque

the fallacy of seeking to defend oneself against a criticism by pointing out that the fault or failing with which one is charged is shared with others.

This common FALLACY, (translated from the Latin as 'you also') is most evident in the context of a debate or discussion. It is sometimes referred to as 'the two wrongs don't make a right fallacy'. Its basic characteristic is that it seeks to dismiss an objection by pointing out that the fault with which it is charged is shared by others as well. The proper conclusion to draw in such a case is that both sides are therefore in the wrong. So there is something self-refuting in the tu quoque strategy.

Consider the following imaginary exchange:

A: 'We need to encourage our employees to cycle to work. Cycling is both healthier and more environmentally friendly.'

B: 'That may be so. But cycling to work can be very dangerous and we shouldn't put the lives of our employees at risk.'

A: 'Well driving to work can be very dangerous too.'

This is a clear example of tu quoque. The ARGUMENT in favour of cycling needs to be defended against the COUNTER-ARGUMENT that it is too dangerous. An adequate defence would seek to provide EVIDENCE to show that it is not so dangerous. Instead the arguer responds by pointing out that other modes of transport, in this case driving, are also dangerous. This response far from defending cycling just concedes the original point that it is dangerous. The proper CONCLUSION to draw is not that cycling is acceptable but that both cycling and driving are, as far as the present reasoning goes, equally unacceptable.

See also: FLAW and INFORMAL FALLACY.

Further reading

Finocchiaro, M. (2005), *Arguments about Arguments*: *Systematic, Critical and Historical Essays in Logical Theory*. Cambridge: Cambridge University Press.

Types of reasoning

Not all reasoning is of the same kind. There are different patterns and strategies and different contexts or subject areas (fields of discourse) suit different styles of argument.

Part of the skill of analysis is in recognizing arguments of different types. The following is a list of those that have entries in this glossary:

- argument from analogy
- argument to the best explanation (abduction)
- causal reasoning
- deduction

- ethical reasoning
- hypothetical reasoning
- induction
- problem solving
- suppositional reasoning
- scientific reasoning
- statistical reasoning
- reductio ad absurdum.

Unwarranted assumption

an assumption, either explicit or more usually implicit, the truth of which is false or at least questionable.

When something has been taken for granted as part of an argument but is either false, or at least highly questionable, then that something is termed an unwarranted assumption.

If the assumption is false then it is easily labelled unwarranted. When the assumption is merely questionable it becomes trickier to determine whether or not the assumption is warranted. In these cases, there is no clear line for distinguishing assumptions from unwarranted assumptions – whether or not an assumption is warranted can sometimes be a matter of judgement. For example, the argument:

> He cannot complain about his punishment. He's admitted to murdering all three school girls and the death penalty is the law in this state.

Here the assumption is that you have no right to complain against a punishment if it is in line with the law. Some people would argue that this belief, or PRINCIPLE, is a fair assumption to make, and therefore warranted; others might disagree.

A flawed argument usually means that there is an unwarranted assumption that is either clearly, or demonstrably, false or, more usually, something that is very likely to be false. For example, take the following argument which makes an obviously fallacious GENERALIZATION:

> Neither Tracy nor Jane like his new shirt. Therefore his new shirt is unlikely to appeal to girls.

Here the unwarranted assumption is that 'All girls will feel the same way about his shirt as do Tracy or Jane', which, without seeing the shirt, is surely very likely to be false.

Note

When an arguer presents an argument with one or more unwarranted assumptions, such as in the given argument, they can also be accused of 'jumping to a CONCLUSION'. The jump describes the step over the missing part of the argument that is deemed to be unwarranted.

See also: ASSUMPTION.

Vagueness

lack of precision or lack of clarity (in language).

Vagueness is different from AMBIGUITY, in that it gives insufficient information in a particular context to be able to identify possible meanings.

For example, consider the following statement:

> We should not legalise euthanasia, because of the problems this would cause for the medical profession.

The phrase 'the problems this would cause for the medical profession' is too vague by itself for us to be able to assess the reasoning contained in the claim. There is no clue in this brief piece of reasoning as to what those problems may be.

Politicians may use vague phrases when they want to impress voters with policies that sound appealing, without being too precise about what the policy involves. They may claim, 'Our tax policies will give maximum reward to hard-working families', without defining 'family' or 'hard-working', and also without specifying what is meant by 'maximum reward' or what the individual members of the family have to do for the family as a whole to be 'hard-working'.

Sometimes people make vague claims because they do not want hearers or readers to know precisely what their intentions are; others may use vague language without intention to deceive but simply because they do not fully understand the topic in question.

It can be more difficult to clarify the meaning of vague language than to clarify ambiguity in language, because there may be no clues in the context to suggest what the meaning could be.

See also: CLARIFYING MEANING.

Validity

in the sense of deductive validity, refers to the relationship between premises and a conclusion so that if the premises are true it is impossible for the conclusion to be false.

An ARGUMENT is deductively valid when the CONCLUSION *has* to follow from the PREMISES. Simple examples of deductively valid arguments include syllogisms and arguments from propositional LOGIC. Thus the following are both examples of deductively valid arguments:

1. All footballers are athletes.
2. All athletes are disciplined.
3. Therefore all footballers are disciplined.

1. If tennis is a sport, then cricket is a sport.
2. Tennis is a sport.
3. Therefore cricket is sport.

What the two arguments have in common, despite their differences of logical form and content, is their validity. In each case the conclusion is certain; it has to follow from the supporting premises.

However, it is important to recognize that validity is not the same as truth. A deductively valid argument can have a false conclusion. It will have a false conclusion if one or more of the premises are false. Validity alone is no guarantee of truth. All that validity determines is that the conclusion does indeed necessarily follow from the premises, but this cannot guarantee the truth of the conclusion if the premises themselves are false. So the following argument, with an obviously false conclusion, is, nevertheless, as valid an argument as the two examples already considered:

1. All footballers are women.
2. All women are daughters.
3. So all footballers are daughters.

Conversely, just as you can have a valid argument with a false conclusion, so you can have an invalid argument with a true conclusion. Consider, for example, the following argument:

1. All footballers are athletes.
2. Some athletes are disciplined.
3. Therefore some footballers are disciplined.

The above argument has a true conclusion, and indeed both premises are true, but nevertheless the conclusion cannot be validly deduced from the premises. Indeed the argument is deductively invalid and an example of a syllogistic fallacy. What this example establishes is that having true premises and a true conclusion is not in itself sufficient for validity; whereas what the previous example shows is that having true premises and a true conclusion is not in itself necessary for validity. Therefore an argument having true premises and a true conclusion is neither necessary nor sufficient for validity; the two concepts are wholly distinct. However, when the two are found together then the argument is classified as SOUND. So a sound argument can be defined as a valid argument with true premises as is arguably the case with the original two examples.

Logic has traditionally been given over to the systematic study of *deductively* valid inferences. The success of logic in codifying and organizing patterns of valid inferences into unified systems has encouraged some to think that all good arguments can be, and should be, properly interpreted, perhaps through some paraphrase and regimentation, as deductively valid arguments. There would be two advantages in doing this. One is that sound arguments would all have the status of PROOFS establishing their conclusions with CERTAINTY. The second is that the underlying logic would provide a perspicuous account of how these arguments all succeed in doing just that. Nevertheless the claim is not plausible and has been challenged from two quarters. First, it has been challenged by those logicians committed to developing inductive logics. An inductive logic aspires like formal deductive logic to codify and systematize valid inferences in purely symbolic terms but unlike formal deductive logic is willing to countenance a different definition of validity in terms of premises raising the PROBABILITY of their conclusions rather than strictly necessitating them. This extended definition of 'validity' to cover inductive inferences is controversial. Second, it has been challenged by INFORMAL LOGICIANS who are sceptical of the value of purely formal systems, whether deductive or inductive, and doubt whether such systems can capture and model all forms of sound reasoning and argumentation conducted in natural languages. This is an ongoing debate but within CRITICAL THINKING there is a consensus that the concept of deductive validity and invalidity is useful for analysing and evaluating only a small and limited number of arguments.

See also: LOGIC, INFORMAL LOGIC, ARGUMENT, SYLLOGISM and SOUND ARGUMENT.

Further reading

Haack, S. (1978), *Philosophy of Logics*. Cambridge: Cambridge University Press.
Read, S. (1995), *Thinking about Logic: An Introduction to the Philosophy of Logic*. Oxford: Oxford University Press.

Value judgement

a judgement as to what is good or bad, right or wrong, important or unimportant.

Value judgements are often referred to as 'subjective' (i.e. relating solely to the mind of the individual) as opposed to objective (i.e. independent of any individual's opinion). Some people have a tendency to dismiss others' arguments simply on the grounds that they rely upon value judgements which, it is claimed, cannot be objective and therefore cannot be the subject of reasoned debate. However, some value judgements rest upon criteria that are not merely subjective. For example, a judgement that an essay is good, or that a tennis player is playing well may be based upon generally accepted criteria.

The categories of value judgement that are most likely to be regarded as mere subjective opinion are aesthetic judgements (e.g. about beauty) and ethical judgements (about moral values). Here are two examples of each:

Aesthetic judgements:

- That is a beautiful painting.
- The taste of caviar is revolting.

Ethical judgements:

- It is wrong to steal from your parents.
- Everyone should give money to charity.

The category of ethical judgements is particularly problematic for CRITICAL THINKING, because although we may be prepared to accept that aesthetic judgements are simply matters of taste about which we do not need to reason, it seems crucial that we should be able to settle ethical questions by reasoned debate. Moreover, all reasoning about what is the right (moral) action or policy depends on value judgements, so if we dismiss all such arguments we exclude ETHICAL REASONING from the sphere of Critical Thinking.

Instead of dismissing such arguments, we should identify the different kinds of claims made (e.g. factual claims and value judgements) and attempt to assess their acceptability by appropriate criteria. To assess factual claims it is appropriate to look for EVIDENCE and judge its RELIABILITY; to assess value judgements we need to consider whether they express an acceptable moral idea, concept or principle. Often there will be no dispute about the acceptability of the moral idea, but dispute may centre on whether the moral idea is applicable to the case under discussion. For example, most people will agree with the value judgement that deliberately harming others is wrong, but may disagree about whether a particular case involves deliberate harm to others. Even if one thinks that there are some ethical issues on which disagreement cannot be resolved rationally, it is important to engage with ethical reasoning to identify the value judgements and seek to work towards agreement.

See also: ETHICAL REASONING, FACT AND OPINION and PRINCIPLE.

Further reading

Thomson, A. (1999), *Critical Reasoning in Ethics*. London: Routledge.

Vested interest

a personal stake in an outcome or decision, such that one stands to gain or lose something important.

Whether or not someone has a vested interest is one criterion for judging their evidence or their arguments. Someone has a vested interest if they would gain something very important by persuading others to reach a particular conclusion or to accept a particular version of events, or if they would lose something very important by failing to do so. Hence a vested interest has the potential to provide someone with a motive to misrepresent the facts.

For example, someone involved in a car accident who was exceeding the speed limit has a vested interest in persuading others that she was driving safely, and thus potentially has a motive for lying about the speed at which she was travelling. A salesman who gets a bonus the size of which depends upon the value of the goods he sells has a vested interest in persuading customers to buy the more expensive products. This may motivate him to overemphasize the reliability of one brand as opposed to another. Scientists engaged in medical research may gain fame and respect if they make a breakthrough in developing an effective and much needed treatment. Hence they may have a vested interest in failing to publish any experimental results that suggest the treatment could have unpleasant side effects.

To say that someone has a vested interest does not mean that they are motivated to misrepresent the facts, nor that they have attempted to do so. Thus although the recognition that someone has a vested interest should make us wary of accepting their claims without corroborating evidence, it should not lead us to assume that they are lying or withholding evidence.

See also: CREDIBILITY and RELIABILITY.

Virtue(s)

character traits, acquired through practice and training, which enable the possessor to excel in those activities which are essential to their flourishing and success.

The simple definition expressed above identifies three core characteristics in the standard Aristotelian conception of a virtue. The first is that virtues are stable, almost permanent characteristics and in this sense differ from other psychological states such as moods, beliefs or desires which can be changeable and need not be long lasting. It is possible to be sad or believe one has a serious illness one day and be elated and believe one is well the next day. But virtues like courage or fair-mindedness or perseverance or honesty insofar as they are genuine do not come and go with each passing moment. Second, virtues are acquired characteristics rather than natural capacities. They presuppose natural capacities but through education, training and upbringing they develop and shape those capacities. Courage is acquired through imitating and practising the behaviour of courageous role models in the course of education and socialization. Third, these acquired characteristics play an essential role in the flourishing and success of those who develop them. Acquired characteristics which play an accidental role in flourishing and success do not count as virtues. So, for example, if someone acquires a character trait of being a buffoon and by chance this wins them the favour of an eccentric millionaire who thereafter provides for all their needs, this does not make being a buffoon into a virtuous characteristic. Virtuous characteristics are characteristics which are, in the *normal* course of things, *necessary* for any being like us, living a life like ours (distinctive of our kind), to be successful and happy.

It is customary, again following Aristotle, to divide virtues, the characteristics normally necessary for beings like us to be successful, into moral and intellectual virtues. The moral virtues are broader than what is normally meant today by the term 'moral'. They essentially refer to all those characteristics necessary to our happiness and success as social beings. Thus Aristotle characterizes being witty as a moral virtue but this does not count as 'moral' in the more limited modern sense of that word. Therefore it is best to think of the so-called moral virtues as social and emotional virtues, where this includes what we might think of as moral virtues (e.g. being fair and truthful) but is not limited to them (e.g. being good at making friends). The intellectual virtues are those permanent characteristics, acquired through upbringing and training, imitation and practice, which are essential to reasoning well both in science (theoretical matters) and ethics and politics (practical matters). The highest of the intellectual virtues for Aristotle is wisdom.

There is widespread agreement that virtues, so understood in this rich and naturalistic sense, should occupy a central place within education. Emphasis on citizenship, on social and emotional intelligence has reawakened interest in the tradition of developing civic and social virtues whereas emphasis on thinking and reasoning skills, and in particular CRITICAL THINKING skills, has also reawakened interest in the Aristotelian tradition of cultivating and educating intellectual, both theoretical and practical, virtues. However, there are many unresolved controversies. One concerns the precise nature of these acquired and permanent characteristics. Some philosophers assimilate the virtues to SKILLS directly, and think of virtues as those skills that are necessary for beings like us, living lives like ours, to be successful and happy. Skill at dribbling a ball, on this view, fails to count as a virtue because it is not normally necessary for human beings to possess this skill to achieve success and fulfilment. Thus Shakespeare, Newton and Beethoven may be supposed, in varying degrees, to have achieved human fulfilment without possessing this skill and insofar as they failed to achieve success and fulfilment it is unlikely that their failure is attributable to the lack of this skill. At best, it is a skill which *happens* to be useful for *some* in certain contingent cultural circumstances to make money but this is not sufficient for it to qualify as a virtue. Aristotle, however, explicitly rejects the identification of virtues with skills. He offers several arguments against their identification. One is that skills are purely instrumental. They are a means to an end. They can be equally well employed in planning a bank robbery as in planning a rescue of earthquake victims. By contrast virtues cannot be used for both good and ill purposes. This is because they are directly involved in the choice of good ends. To be truthful is to choose the truth for its own sake, something that one values intrinsically, irrespective of what one may or may not get out of it for oneself. A lying dossier can be produced by someone possessed of some skills in the manipulation of arguments and evidence but not by someone with the virtue of truthfulness.

For this reason some philosophers have assimilated virtues to dispositions where the dispositions are essentially motivational and stand behind the skills as making use of them in the pursuit of certain ends. So on this view the education of a critical thinker involves not simply the development of certain skills in developing and handling arguments and evidence but also the fostering of appropriate motivations or dispositions which are identified with virtues. Typically these will include dispositions such as FAIR-MINDEDNESS, open-mindedness, perseverance, love of truth, curiosity and intellectual courage. Thus a critical thinker is not simply a skilled thinker but a skilled thinker with the right motivations. This is an elegant solution. However, it has an unattractive dualism at its heart, a dualism of reason and appetite, made graphic and explicit in Hume's notorious dictum that 'Reason is, and ought only to be, the slave of the passions and should never pretend to any other office whatsoever'. What this means is that reason or skill can effect the means but the choice of ends belongs not to reason or skill but to our non-cognitive motivations and dispositions. So understood this renders reason wholly instrumental, hence its easy assimilation to skill, and as purely instrumental, reason is in a position to satisfy antecedent motives but not in a position to critically reflect upon which motives or dispositions education should promote. In Hume's striking phrase it is 'the slave of the passions', their tool or instrument in devising plans and stratagems for overcoming obstacles which prevent their satisfaction.

One way through this impasse, favoured by contemporary defenders of the significance and importance of the virtues, is to see the virtues as acquired characteristics to accept and endorse certain values and norms. So being truthful is a matter of genuinely valuing the truth where this valuation arises out of the education and formation of natural capacities. Similarly being fair-minded involves being willing to listen to and think about arguments and evidence for positions contrary to one's own dearly held views. However, these virtues which then guide REASONING and thinking can be supported and justified by the very thinking and reasoning which they make possible. This proposal involves circularity in that reasoning and thinking can both be guided by norms and values and also provide some critical defence of those norms and values. It is not clear whether this is defensible or not. What is clear is that educational research is currently centred on questions of skills, dispositions and virtues, and the interrelationship between them and will remain so for some time to come.

See also: SKILL and CRITICAL THINKING.

Further reading

Mcdowell, J. (1979), 'Virtue and reason'. *The Monist*, lxii, 331–50.
Zagzebski,L. T. (1996), *Virtues of the Mind: An Inquiry into the Nature of Virtue and the Ethical Foundations of Knowledge.* Cambridge: Cambridge University Press.

List of Entries

A to Z of Critical Thinking

abduction

ad hoc

ad hominem

affirming the consequent

allegation

ambiguity

analogy (argument from)

analysis

anecdotal evidence

appeals

appeal to authority/expertise

appeal to emotion/pity/anger/fear etc.

appeal to history/precedent

appeal to popularity

appeal to tradition

argument

argument indicator

argument structure

argument (inference) to the best explanation

argument versus explanation

assertion

assessment

assumption

begging the question

bias

causal explanation

cause and effect

certainty

chain of reasoning
circularity; circular reasoning
claim
clarifying meaning
coherence
complex arguments
conclusion
conditional statement
conflation
consistency
contradiction
converse
correlation
corroboration
counter-argument
counter-assertion
creative thinking
credibility
Critical Thinking

deduction / deductive reasoning
definition
denying the antecedent
dilemma

empirical/empiricism
epistemology
equivocation
ethical reasoning
evaluation
evidence
example
expertise
explanation
extracting an argument

fact and opinion
fairmindedness
fallacy, formal

fallacy, informal (GW/JB)
false dichotomy
false dilemma
flaw

generalization
grounds

hearsay
hypothesis
hypothetical induction
hypothetical reasoning

imply
inconsistency
independent reasoning
induction
inference / infer
inference to the best explanation
informal fallacy
informal logic (GW/BB)
intermediate conclusion
irrelevance

joint reasoning
judgement
justification

knowledge, theory of

logic

mean
measures of central tendency
median
metacognition
mistaking necessary and sufficient conditions
mode
modus ponens and modus tollens
moral reasoning